To Lois
Peace

Doctor
Bob Lee
107.5
WBLS

We must be the change that we want to see in the World.
—**Mahatma Gandhi**

Praise
For Doctor Bob Lee and Make the Grade Foundation

There is a passage of scripture (Gen 50:20) that states, *You intended to harm me, but God intended it for good to accomplish what is now being done, the saving of many lives.* These words sum up Dr. Bob Lee's vision and mission presented in *7 Ways To Make The Grade.* Countless times his life could have ended by wrong turns, childhood mischief or tragic mishaps. I am a lifetime youth developer and I recognize the heart and soul of a youth warrior. Bob Lee did not allow fame or fortune to deter him from helping others. He worked on his life with the encouragement of his parents and mentors. From humble beginnings in Queensbridge Public Housing, he would later meet giants in the recording industry, mayors, civil rights leaders and even presidents. Dr. Bob Lee never let go of the strong loving hand that guided him down the darkest alleys of life. He took his near knockout lesson from his early days as a boxer and now he is knocking out the issues trying to take young people out! I am proud to be a brother, colleague and friend, witnessing firsthand Bob Lee's awesome giving spirit, joy of life, and desire to not only make a difference but also be the difference. Bob Lee was called to save many lives through sharing wise and practical foundational precepts. I can say with all assuredness—Dr. Bob Lee, You Have Made The Grade!

—**Rev. Dr. Alfonso Wyatt, Founder,**
Strategic Destiny: Designing Futures Through Faiths & Facts

Our ancestors were right on point when they said, "It takes a village to raise a child." Dr. Bob Lee echoes these sentiments in his book, *7 Ways to Make the Grade.* In order to effectively educate a child, it demands a multidimensional approach. It requires thinking outside of the status quo, meeting the needs of the students, and empowering them to find their purpose in life. We must help our young people to establish goals and assist them in developing a plan, which will support them in reaching their highest potential. It is crucial that young people understand that making the grade is not just about what they achieve today, it is more about how making the grade will ultimately impact their tomorrow.

—**Dr. Arnette F. Crocker**
Principal, Women's Academy of Excellence

I would like to truly thank you on behalf of the Howard University Association of Black Journalists. We had an awesome time at WBLS! Thank you for giving us this opportunity. I know that all the students walked away learning something new. Above everything, the students all said our time spent at WBLS encouraged them to never give up. Seeing the successes of all the professionals in your office made them realize their dreams can become reality. I cannot thank you enough for organizing the tour and discussions. We are truly grateful. We look forward to working with you in the future. Thank you.

—Mary Godie, HUABJ President 2009-2010

"Doctor Bob Lee, in a single word, Effervescent! Over the years, I witnessed Doctor Bob Lee's abundant excitement about life, the life he wanted to live, and the life he knew that our children could have. The possibilities he felt could be captured through hard work, commitment, and education. I witnessed the effervescence captivate and capture the hearts and minds of young people. This young man among men, proud, navigating his ever-changing fate without malice of thought in his chosen world simply called "media" never lost sight of his signature smile, voice and that cup of care always in his back pocket for each and every child that crossed his path.

The last essences of summer brush my cheek. I inhale thick and colorful aromas of autumn. It is back to school time. It is Doctor Bob Lees' time. I think back to the days when he would pull up to public schools in the WBLS Van and work his magic. Doctor Bob Lee left every child eager to go to school. Young people paid attention to his public service announcements and they got it. I called it magic because Bob Lee connected. He built a strong, motivational bridge with one direction—*straight into young spirits and minds.* Today, our best educators and an arsenal of millions of dollars can't seem to quite hit the mark, not in the way Doctor Bob Lee did.

I applaud the good works of Make the Grade Foundation and I hope that everyone reads, "7 Ways to Make the Grade." This book is long overdue for the massive volume of good work that Doctor Bob Lee has done throughout the years; it deserves to be chronicled. I am sure that this new book will be an empowering guide for all of us. I only hope that Doctor Lee continues his journey and shares more of his life experiences, for he has a monumental body of work in his photography.

If you haven't guessed by now, I am a longtime admirer and fan of Doctor Bob Lee. Bob, I send you peace, blessings and best wishes for abundant success as you continue to take care of our children, our future."

—Lynnette C. Velasco, Author, Zinzi: A Child's Journey to
Self-Fulfillment, Giving and CaringPoet, Essayist
and Special Assistant to NYC Council Member Inez E. Dickens

7 WAYS TO MAKE THE GRADE

A LIVING GUIDE TO YOUR COMMUNITY'S SUCCESS!
PARENTS, TEACHERS, STUDENTS, COMMUNITY,
CLERGY, HEALTH & FINANCIAL LITERACY

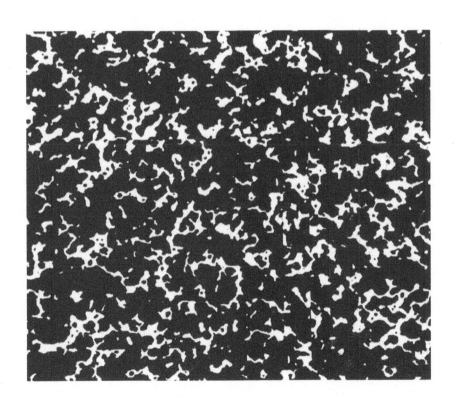

7 WAYS TO MAKE THE GRADE

A LIVING GUIDE TO YOUR COMMUNITY'S SUCCESS!
PARENTS, TEACHERS, STUDENTS, COMMUNITY,
CLERGY, HEALTH & FINANCIAL LITERACY

BY DOCTOR BOB LEE
With Yvonne Rose

BOB LEE ENTERPRISES
New York City

7 WAYS TO MAKE THE GRADE

Published by:
Make the Grade Publishing
244 Madison Avenue, #500
New York, NY 10016
Phone: (212) 459-4696
boblee@makethegrade.org
www.makethegrade.org
Bob Lee, Publisher & Editorial Director
Yvonne Rose, Editor
QualityPress.info, Production Coordinator
Printed Page, Interior & Cover Layout

Make the Grade Foundation Books are available at special discounts for bulk purchases, sales promotions, fund raising or educational purposes.

DEDICATION
To The Bright Memory of:

My Loving Father, John Robert Lee
Who would always say, _"Stay in school, be on time and be sure to get a good education!"_ As a child, I can remember placing my little hand, into his hands, especially in times of fear, which led to my belief and faith that my father is always watching over me.

My Sister Ida Lacy,
An extraordinary woman and my biggest fan and critique, who watched me on television and listened to me on radio. You taught me the gift of playing music, motivated me and helped me to believe that I can do anything I put my mind to.

An Incredible Teacher · Mentor · Friend, Hal Jackson
Who taught me the importance of Community Service, he would often say, _"It's nice to be important, but it's more important to be nice."_ Hal's wisdom, compassion and mentorship helped me to realize the importance of community service and allowed me to understand that everyone I would meet would be important to me.

Acknowledgements

To The Many People Who Have Given Their Time and Support to the building of The Make the Grade Foundation. I give special thanks to:

Current Board of Directors

Lianna Lee, LCSW-R, CASAC

Shiheim Wilson Lee, *International Educator*

Debi Jackson, *Co-Host of Hal Jackson's Sunday Classics (WBLS)*

Shekire Rodriguez, RN *and U.S. Navy Veteran*

Denise Rogers, *Vice President of Marketing · Public Relations*

Anthony Harmon, *Community Affairs Director, United Federation of Teachers*

Ann Tripp, *Nationwide News Correspondent of the Steve Harvey Morning Show*

Marvin Holland, Director, Political Action, Transport Workers Union Local 100

Verdia Noel, Area Director, Council for Airport Opportunity, Inc.

Darryl J. Mack, Assistant Principal, NYC Department of Education

Dr. Donna Williams, Owner, Morningside Dental Care, PC

Advisory Board Members

Dr. Roscoe C. Brown, Jr., One of The Original Tuskegee Airmen, *Director of the Center for Urban Education Policy; University Professor, Graduate School and University Center of The City University of New York*

Hazel Dukes, *President of the NAACP New York State Conference Member of the NAACP National Board of Directors*

Voza Rivers, *Chairman/CEO VOZ Entertainment Group; Executive Producer/Founding Member, New Heritage Theatre Group, Co-Founder Executive Producer, IMPACT Repertory Theatre*

Elinor Tatum, *Publisher and Editor in Chief of the New York Amsterdam News, The oldest and largest black newspaper in the City of New York, One of the oldest **ethnic papers** in the Country*

Legal Advisors

Robb W. Patryk, Partner, Hughes Hubbard & Reed LLP

Natasha N. Reed, Counsel, Hughes Hubbard & Reed LLP

I offer my sincerest gratitude to past and present Make the Grade Foundation Board Members

Verdia M. Nol, Area Director, Council for Airport Opportunity, Inc,; Lianna Lee, LCSW-R, CASAC Director of Behavioral Health Services at Elmcor Youth & Adult Activities, Inc.; Lou Benson, Board Member & Former Director of Rehabilitation for Elmcor Youth and Adult Activities, Inc.; Hon. Randolph Jackson, Justice of the Supreme Court (ret'd); Shiheim Wilson Lee, High School Physical Education: IB Sports, Exercise and Health Science , Jakarta Intercultural School; Shekire Rodriquez; Charles Sessoms; and our lawyer & adviser, Robb Patryk, Partner, Hughes, Hubbard & Reed, LLP; Debi Jackson; Natasha Reed, Esq.; Kernie L. Anderson, April Raven Bobyn; Elaine Edmonds; Randa Guastella; Mac McDonald; Aaron Morgan; Asiyah Ray; Willie Walker Ade Williams; Ayo Sanderson-Wilson; Anthony Harmon; Denise Rogers; Ann Tripp; Kenneth M. Wilson, PsyD; and to public relations/event coordinators Phyllis M. Shelton and Cassandra Ramirez.

I also gratefully acknowledge all of you, who have been factors to the success of Make the Grade Foundation, including our *Elected Officials, Sponsors, Educators, Parents, Students, Health Care Providers, Media, Friends, Associates, Community and Faith-Based Organization*s.

For the wonderful remarks from those who contributed to the content of *7 Ways to Make the Grade,* including: Ryan Mack, Financial Entrepreneur & CNN Commentator; J. R. Peter Nelson, Ph.D., former CEO, Joseph P. Addabbo Family Health Center; Hon. Randolph Jackson, Justice of the Supreme Court (ret'd); Mark S. Brantley, Esq., Chairman of the Board, Municipal Credit Union; Leah Lakins, Owner and Editor-in-Chief, Fresh Eyes Editorial Services; Tony Rose, Publisher/CEO of Amber Communications Group, Inc.; and Yvonne Rose, Director of Quality Press for defining the necessary steps to complete this book.

To my family for understanding my passions and standing behind me on each and every journey I have taken.

Contents

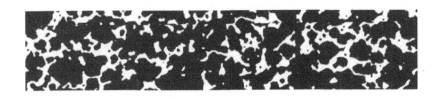

Foreword

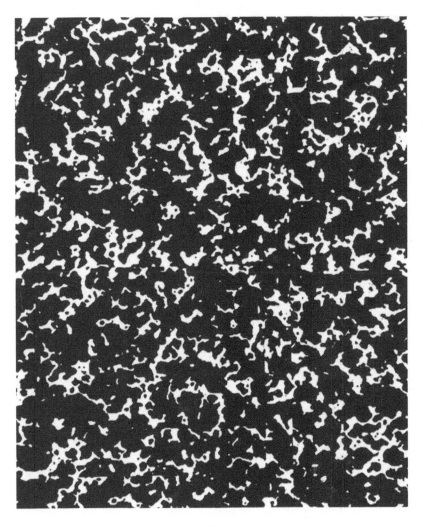

INNOVATION IS HOW I SURVIVED and HOW I MADE THE GRADE

As a young child, Books, Music and the love of God saw me through the darkest moments of my life. I visited the Bookmobile on a regular basis, learned to swim at the Boys Club, became a paperboy at the Bay State Banner and the Christian Science Monitor, visited my Grandma in the suburbs, served as an Altar Boy at church and began my formal education at a Catholic school. As I reflect back, I realize that all these activities garnered me positive adult mentoring experiences, which contributed to my escape from the clutches of the law and helped me to MAKE THE GRADE.

Like Bob Lee, I, also experienced the evils of growing up in a concrete jungle aka the housing projects, but unlike him, I was a product of a single-parent household. I was born in Roxbury (Boston) Massachusetts, raised in the Whittier Street Housing Projects, honorably discharged from the U.S. Air Force after serving in the Vietnam War, and attended the University of Massachusetts and the University of California in Los Angeles. I later became a world-renowned record producer with production deals on Virgin and Atlantic Records, and an NAACP Image Award winning book publisher.

Innovation was a survival tactic for me. I grew up understanding that one has to be innovative and come up with a new way to survive, a new way to live, a new idea or thought process that can move you from one place to another, a new way of doing things...whether it's getting credit at the grocery store to eat, or selling newspapers, or shining shoes, or holding down two buildings with customers that you can rely on to go to the store for, to run their numbers or to get anything they need. I began to find ways to innovate and to be unusual with that.

It's a long way from the Whittier Street Housing Projects to becoming an NAACP Image Award Winner, and a lot of amazing people saw that child, that teenager, and guided and helped him on that journey.

Outside of winning one of the most prestigious awards that has ever been bestowed upon African Americans, a personal accomplishment probably would be that the successes of those things and those visions that have succeeded through hard and smart work...through working with great people, great minds, understanding those minds and people that come into my world and being allowed to enter other worlds to see that.

They're called "Dreams come true" and that's what we must always try to obtain...a dream that can come true, a dream that can better help the lives of others, including your own. By following your dream, by believing in yourself and in God, you can and will find your purpose, and you will MAKE THE GRADE.

I have great respect for people who can come from great adversity, bad parents, bad schools, and bad environments and turn their lives into something in spite of that. So, I guess that's the major accomplishment, and from then on, it's to make sure that you don't fall back into a negative lifestyle whereby you cannot accomplish and cannot work.

Tens of millions of African American people get up and go to work every day. They're accomplishing and feeding their families and taking care of their children, and they mind the law and the rule of thumb. They are my heroes. So I guess the accomplishment always is "Can you be a better person from whence you came?" And if you come from better, Can you maintain that and do better for others? So, I guess the number one accomplishment would be accomplishing in a place where good and evil co-exist, side by side.

Bob Lee has spent the majority of his life paying it forward, mentoring young people and giving back to the community through his Make the Grade Foundation. 7 Ways to Make the Grade elaborates on the organization's collaboration between parents, teachers, students, clergy, community, health care professionals and financial literacy Instructors.

I invite all of you to take a second look at the kids in your community. If you feel that a child is experiencing difficulties or pain, you may not be able to change their environment, but you can give him or her something to dream about—a goal to strive for—a way of knowing that there is another life beyond the one they are currently trapped in. Whoever can dream and hold onto hope...those are the winners... the ones who will MAKE THE GRADE.

Tony Rose

Publisher/CEO, Amber Communications Group, Inc.

2013 NAACP Image Award Winner for Outstanding Literary Work

2013 Phillis Wheatley Publisher of the Year

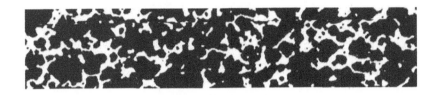

Introduction

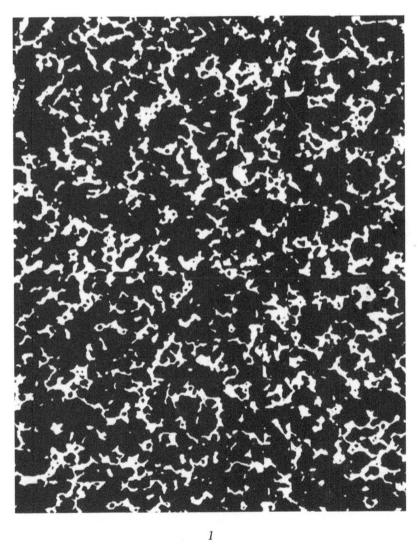

Learning gives creativity,
Creativity leads to thinking,
Thinking provides knowledge,
Knowledge makes you great.

—Abdul Kalam

As we drove through the suburbs with my dad, he would point out beautiful homes and big pretty cars and would say, "That's a pretty house and a fine car…" On those long road trips with my dad, the words I heard impacted my childhood and encouraged me to dream about a brighter future. He would always encourage us with positive statements, such as: "There's power in knowledge. If you get a good education you can tell them what you want and won't have to accept what they want to give you. You can have all of this, if you stay in school, study hard and stay out of trouble." That was my dad—my hero, my namesake, John Robert Lee—talking to me.

Although, I was just one of the seven children crowded into our family station wagon on those long drives to the country, it always felt like my father was speaking directly to me. It was actually an educational experience for all of us. We listened attentively and observed what nature had to offer. Cows, horses, deer, chickens, the road seemed to stretch to the ends of the earth, and those houses… Wow! My family and I couldn't wait to pile into the car and see all that, again and again; I couldn't get enough of it. I always remembered those outings, the beautiful landscapes, and the pleasures associated with freedom and fresh air. I took all that in and whenever I stepped out of line and trouble reared its ugly head, I turned around and took a different path.

I grew up in one of the many concrete jungles dropped into urban New York's ghettos, the housing projects, where to this day, only the strong-willed can survive. It was instilled in me that I would be one of the survivors, a leader, a teacher and a role model to all who would listen…and it worked. My father's words and his concern for my well-being were the main contributors that helped shape me into the man I am today.

Looking back, I can't put my finger on just one person who inspired me, but rather a community of people: family members, friends, teachers and mentors who took an interest in me during my youth and throughout my adulthood. Eventually, I evolved into "Doctor" Bob Lee, Entrepreneur, Consultant and On-Air Radio personality at WBLS 107.5 (New York City), and Host for "OPEN" on Bronxnet Television (Bronx, New York).

In 1986, I founded Bob Lee Enterprises, an Entertainment company with the help of another radio personality, "Morning Man Ken Spider Webb" In 2004, my dream of forming an educational foundation was born, "Make the Grade Foundation for Education". I wanted the name of the foundation to be meaningful and to support the key components that could serve and strengthen communities by forming a collaboration between parents, teachers, students, community, clergy, health care, and financial literacy professionals.

Clearly, a major part of my thinking, as I continue to try to help other people get what they need out of life, is that I had to link a book up to Make the Grade Foundation. I came up with *7 Ways to Make the Grade*, a motivational inspirational self-help book written to advise and guide young people in their quest to make the grade and become successful in their journey through life.

And, no matter what your journey is, always remember this…What you are is God's Gift to you and what you make of yourself is your gift to God; so choose your choice and let your choice control the chooser.

—Bob Lee

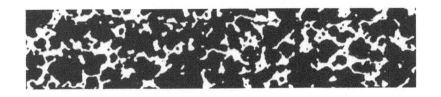

Part One

Building My Foundation

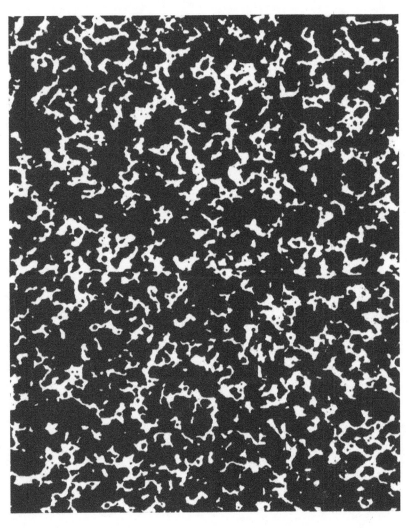

CHAPTER ONE

Make the Grade Foundation— In the Beginning

Opportunities don't happen, you create them.
                                                    —Chris Grosser

When you have on the armor of education, you are not only affording yourself power and opportunity, but you are also declaring that you have what it takes to make the grade.

Several years ago, I had wanted to start an educational organization called the Bob Lee Foundation for Education; however, most people usually use their names and I wanted to put a more meaningful name on my foundation, referencing what it stands for.

The idea came to me one day in the shower of my home. I suddenly jumped out, scuffled across the floor, slipping and sliding. I grabbed a pen and paper and started writing the names. What I pictured in my mind were students wearing graduation caps, traveling uphill on a long winding road. They climbed a long ladder up to the sky while reaching for a star. To me, it sent a message of young people striving for something they believed could be obtained, dreaming big…making the grade. I believe that no matter how long it takes, *if you stick with something long enough, something always happens.*

After much contemplation and thinking about all the factors that I felt would make a difference to the young people I would be reaching, I decided on the name "Make the Grade Foundation". It seemed to fit well and all the pieces of my puzzle could now work together as a unit. I visualized a group of people giving helping hands. It was so perfect—parent, student, teacher, community, clergy, health care, and financial literacy.

In December 2004 I founded The Make the Grade Foundation for Education (MTG), a non-profit organization that facilitates and encourages academic achievement by implementing programs to tutor, mentor and motivate students, while providing incentives and funding. MTG enhances the educational experience of young people through collaboration with students, parents, educators, clergy, the community, health care, and financial literacy. Programs include: The Communications program where we build Internet radio and TV Stations at community based organizations, schools, churches and community centers in order to teach students how to present themselves and how to communicate well, In addition we have the MTG Mentoring and Tutoring Programs, Shadow Programs, Partnering with Parents and we also offer some College Scholarships. We like to partner with many like-minded community programs, schools and organizations.

Although our programs are primarily focused on schools in the New York Tri-state area, I was heavily influenced by educational practices that I saw when I visited South Africa. During this trip, I gained a better idea of what was needed to make students successful. The schools in South Africa reminded me of my youth and what I experienced during my school days. Back then, teachers were very accessible and had an open relationship that enabled them to discipline children within reason. My teachers didn't hesitate to call my parents when they felt it was necessary. I wanted to instill this same level of community into the Make the Grade Foundation. I realized that when you are equipped with an education, an opportunity, a mentor and a purpose, you can begin to lay the foundation to get whatever you want out of life.

In addition to my father, I was blessed to have Hank Carter as a coach and mentor during my youth. Hank is the founder of the Wheelchair Charities, and he instilled in me the discipline to take on the necessary actions to become successful. He also taught me about paying it forward and looking out for people in need. He currently buys motorized beds, wheelchairs, and computers for people in wheelchairs. Hank Carter was like another parent in the community who looked out for all of us; I was lucky that our paths crossed.

When I was growing up, I was fortunate to have many wonderful neighbors who, like Hank, looked out for me. It was commonplace for a neighbor to say to another, "Hey, keep an eye on my kid," or "If he acts up, don't be afraid to pull him aside and reprimand him." There was no shame with other adults in the community keeping every kid in our neighborhood in line. It was commonplace that you could receive a spanking from everybody, from your mother's best friend to an elderly congregant at your church. Then when you got home your mother or father would make you cut a switch or get a belt and whip you again. We never got away with much of anything.

The discipline even extended from our church, even if you weren't a member. The pastor at the church would be quick to call your parents to have a conference if they saw you causing trouble in the neighborhood. He would put forth the effort to intervene and speak to your parents about your behavior, regardless of whether it was good, bad, or indifferent.

My goal with the Make the Grade Foundation was to restore that sense of community that is missing in today's society. You can't reprimand a youngster today like people did in the past. I knew that we needed more extended families and community outreach to increase the layers of concern surrounding each child. For more than 20 years, while working with WBLS & WLIB in NY, I had visited numerous organizations and schools throughout the Tri-State area, mentoring Youth and families. Not knowing quite what it would be, I prayed through the calmness and quiet, I visualized an organization that could tie all the necessary entities together.

I recognized the importance of establishing an organization that would focus on the collaboration between parent, teacher, student, community, and clergy. Later on, we added a financial literacy and healthy living component. In order to help the young people learn better, we needed to stress health in regards to healthy eating and healthy living....both physically and mentally

I had been visiting schools in the mornings with the WBLS "On Time Program". It was a community service program sponsored intermittently by Pepsi, Burger King, and the American Dairy

Associates. We also did a TV commercial to make sure students and families knew that they could have free breakfast or lunch in school.

The WBLS "On Time Program" helped to mold me into doing what I do now with the Make the Grade Foundation. I had finally laid the groundwork and established my mission, based on the collaboration of hundreds of caring people, who could make up an awesome team. But it was a long effort. We began to get the ball rolling after a housing expo at the Jacob Javit's Convention Center, where we were teaching people how to do everything all under one roof—how to buy a house, how to finance, how to do closing—and all the steps that went into home ownership. There, I met an attorney who was interested in working with CBOs (Community-based organizations) dealing with education. After numerous meetings, planning and research, we launched the Make the Grade Foundation.

Around that time, a young lady named Asia Ray kept calling me to follow up on what I had told her about starting a foundation. She was interested in working with me on it and remained persistent. She said, "We need to start this now! Let's make it happen!" Perhaps, she was more serious than I was at the time, and I was very serious. Asia was enthusiastic and determined—just what I needed to keep the ball rolling.

In addition, we have many gifted Make the Grade Foundation partners and volunteers from the corporate and local communities who have the ability to connect with people. The volunteers regularly help with fundraising, mentoring, and visiting schools. Together we make presentations focused on encouraging academic progress and commitment to excellence.

I began to ask other people to become involved in the Make the Grade Foundation project and ultimately pulled together a team of concerned people, who like myself, wanted to steer people in the right direction.

Two of the Founding Advisory Board Members: Hal Jackson and Percy Sutton, who were at the top of my list, are unfortunately, both deceased. Hal and Percy understood the value of a good education and a healthy start…and they made sure that I would follow suit.

Hal Jackson was always in the community interacting with people and I wanted to be just like him. Hal began his broadcasting career as the first African-American radio sports announcer, broadcasting Howard University's home baseball games and local Negro League Baseball games. *Howard University's students still visit the station today with the Make the Grade Foundation Shadow Program.*

Hal Jackson's broadcasting career spanned eight decades; he continued to host *Sunday Classics* on WBLS each Sunday at 6 pm with Clay Berry and his wife—Deborah Bolling Jackson—who is known professionally as 'Debi B'. Hal was on the air until just three weeks prior to his death on May 23, 2012.

Hal Jackson was the first African American host at WINX/Washington with *The Bronze Review*, a nightly interview program. He later hosted *Talk Show*, a program of jazz and blues on WOOK-TV. In 1954 Hal became the first radio personality to broadcast three daily shows on three different New York stations. Hal Jackson received numerous accolades for being an industry leader, among them becoming the first minority inducted into the National Association of Broadcaster's Hall of Fame and the first African-American inducted into the Radio Hall of Fame. He was also given a Pioneer Award by the Rhythm and Blues Foundation in 2003 and in October 2010, the Library of American Broadcasting named Hal a "Giant in Broadcasting".

In 1971, Hal Jackson and Percy Sutton co-founded the Inner City Broadcasting Corporation (ICBC), which acquired WLIB — making it the first African-American owned-and-operated station in New York. The following year, ICBC acquired WLIB-FM, and changed its call letters to WBLS ("the total Black experience in Sound").

While talking to Hal Jackson, he told me that he was one of five children, and was orphaned at the age of eight. He spent much of his youth raising himself and was even homeless at one time, but managed to find odd jobs to keep himself clothed, fed, and housed. Despite his rocky start, Hal Jackson went on to become a broadcast giant and a legend; but he never forgot from whence he came. Hal was always in the community interacting with people and I wanted to be just like him. In 1970 he founded the Hal Jackson Talented Teens International Scholarship Competition a national talent contest and scholarship award program for girls between the ages of 13 and

16 years old that I had the honor and pleasure of co-hosting from 1984–2010.

Percy Sutton had always been interested in having the radio personnel visit the schools. He was one of my most important role models, who along with Hal Jackson had brought me aboard as an Inner City Broadcasting intern. I owe much of my current status to both of these great and prominent men.

Percy Sutton was born in San Antonio, Texas. November 24, 1920 and he succumbed December 26, 2009. He was the last of fifteen children and no stranger to the needs of a large family, the relevance of entrepreneurship, the hard work associated with it and the rewards earned from being in charge of your own destiny.

At age twelve, Percy stowed away on a passenger train to New York City, New York, where he slept under a sign on 155th Street in the Harlem neighborhood of the Manhattan borough of the city. His family was committed to civil rights, and even as a child, Percy sought out opportunities that would contribute to the success of "the movement". At age thirteen, while passing out leaflets in an all-white neighborhood for the National Association for the Advancement of Colored People (NAACP), a policeman beat Percy, but that didn't quiet his spirit. He joined the Boy Scouts of America and attained the rank of Eagle Scout in 1936 at the age of sixteen; and years later, at which time Percy stated that scouting was a key factor in shaping his life, he was recognized with the Distinguished Eagle Scout Award

During World War II, Percy Sutton served as an intelligence officer with the Tuskegee Airmen along with Roscoe C. Brown, one of the other Make the Grade Advisory Board members. Percy Sutton won combat stars in both the Italian and Mediterranean theaters. During the 1950s and 1960s, Percy became one of America's best-known lawyers, representing many controversial figures, such as Malcolm X. He initiated the revitalization of the Apollo Theater in Harlem and co-produced *It's Showtime at the Apollo*, a syndicated, music television show that first broadcast on September 12, 1987.

While talking to Mr. Sutton, one day, he told me how important it was to be diversified in business, stating, "You know, Bob, I always keep four or five businesses because if one or two fail I'm still in business." Percy Sutton knew how important education was in our community and backed the edification of young minds in every way; he thought the WBLS On Time program was a great community service.

When I formed the Make the Grade Foundation, because they had experienced many ups and downs and came through much adversity, Hal Jackson and Percy Sutton were very relevant to my way of thinking. It took a lot to get to where they were going, but they persevered. Both Hal and Percy made the grade and became legends in their own right. If you define your purpose, learn from your mistakes and find great role models, your journey toward making the grade will be a lot easier.

No matter what you do in life, *always* keep it real with yourself. Being honest about who you are and your circumstances will keep your mind focused and your feet sure. You can't change anyone but yourself, so acknowledge your position for *exactly* what it is, accept it no matter how much it hurts, and then take steps to improve your situation. I have come to realize that the way to do that is through education, hard work, dedication, and determination. Begin to try to help yourself before you can help others.

7 WAYS TO MAKE THE GRADE

1. I believe that no matter how long it takes, *if you stick with something long enough, something always happens.*

2. When you have on the armor of education, you are not only affording yourself power and opportunity, but you are also declaring that you have what it takes to make the grade.

3. Equipped with an education, an opportunity and a purpose, you can begin to lay the foundation to get whatever you want out of life and help others do the same.

4. I think that a caring family, friends and neighbors are some of the things that are missing today—some of the things that would keep young people in line.

5. If you define your purpose, learn from your mistakes and find great role models, your journey toward making the grade will be a lot easier.

6. Being honest about whom you are and your circumstances will keep your mind focused and your feet sure.

7. You can't change anyone but yourself, so acknowledge your position for *exactly* what it is, accept it no matter how much it hurts, and then take steps to improve your situation.

CHAPTER TWO

From Whence I Came

The meaning of life is to find your gift.
The purpose of life is to give it away.
—Anonymous

John Robert Lee, Jr. was my given name; but everyone called me Bobby Lee. I embarked upon the game of life on March 27, 1956 when my mom Anna Lee welcomed me into the world at the St. John's Hospital in Elmhurst, Queens. My dad, John Robert Lee, who was my namesake was right by my mom's side.

Anna who was born in Naples, Italy in the town of Abelino, experienced first-hand, the ravages of World War II when, as a teenager, she volunteered for the Italian Red Cross. Anna was a war bride who had met, fallen in love with and married an American soldier, Robert Harper. When Anna was seventeen-years-old, she and Robert had their first child, my brother Tommy, who was born in Naples, Italy. When she was eighteen years old, Anna moved to the United States with her husband and son where their family eventually migrated to Saint Louis, Missouri. My sister Ida was born, and soon after, Robert succumbed to war wounds, leaving a devastated young widow to raise two children alone.

My mom was a beautiful young woman, with long jet-black curly hair that cascaded down her back. Her 5'2" frame was quite shapely and perfectly proportioned; and her radiant smile attracted many admirers. She was a waitress at a small diner near the railroad station when she met my father, who answered to the nickname "Red" given to him by his friends.

Red was of average stature and had reddish-brown hair, which he marceled to make it wavy. He was African American mixed with Native American and had sort of a red-tan looking skin tone. He was born in Columbus, Ohio and eventually moved to New York City, where he landed a job as a Pullman Porter and waiter on the New York Grand Central Railroad trains. Red used to travel all across the country and maintained that job for many years. St. Louis was one of the stops on the railroad and whenever he was in town, one of Red's favorite places to eat at was the diner where Anna worked. He became one of her regular customers and after a while, they started dating. Red fell in love with Anna's warm and welcoming personality.

My dad knew that my mother was a widow with two kids. He enjoyed bringing them gifts and helping her take care of them, whenever she needed help. Eventually they became a couple and got married. He moved my mother, my brother Tommy and my sister Ida to live in Harlem, New York. Soon after, Lianna was born, followed by me, and my three brothers—Cliff, Tony, and Eddie. I always got excited when my dad would come home from his railroad job. He used to pull out all of his tips, dump a bunch of change on the table and tell us to "pick up, pick up," which meant we could pick up some of the change.

My mother was a wonderful, caring woman and she could cook really well, offering great traditional Italian meals—like spaghetti and meatballs, lasagna, pizza, and eggplant parmesan. However, she also learned from my dad and some friends, and became an expert at cooking succulent Southern Cuisine, using their family recipes. I remember the great fried chicken, black eyed peas, collard greens, pig knuckles, candied yams, macaroni and cheese, potato salad, pinto beans, and so much more—she made the best meals. *We had two different grease cans on the stove—one for the fish and one for the chicken.* And then there were those great deserts—chocolate layer cake, sweet potato pie, coconut cake, and banana pudding.

I was just two years old when my brother Cliff was born, but at that young age I witnessed my mother giving birth to him on the living room couch and still retain that image. I didn't quite know what was going on, but I do remember some neighbors trying to assist her. That black and red couch stayed in the family for some time afterward, and was a reminder of Cliff's very special new beginning.

A few years after Cliff was born, Dad decided to stay in one location instead of traveling on the railroad, so he got a job as a doorman at an apartment building in Forest Hills, Queens. My mother was very dedicated to maintaining the family structure. She spent most of her time caring for her seven children; but as we got older, she worked part-time as a school aide for the public school system. Dad was sensitive, hardworking, and strong. I resembled him in all the principles he stood for. He was a fast walker, walking to stay in shape, always telling us, "Move your body". We had to almost run to keep up with him, Dad was always very health-conscious and remained in great physical condition, still walking in his nineties. He passed away in 1995 at age 95. My parents remained together until that day. In 2015 my mother celebrated her 85th birthday.

One day, when I was about 7 or 8-years-old, my world as I knew it, would change and I was thrown into confusion. It began when Uncle Buddy was walking from the train station to the Queensbridge Projects. He had been drinking and decided he was going to tell Cliff and me about this big secret he had been keeping for years. When he spotted us in the playground, he called us over. We greeted him the same as always, shouting out: "Uncle Buddy! Uncle Buddy!"

Without hesitation, He said with a thick tongue and a slur, "Boys, I've got something to tell ya!" As we continued to walk up the block with him towards my building, he shouted one of the biggest life-changing statements I would ever hear, "BOYS! I'M YOUR FATHER!"

I didn't know what just hit me or didn't know what to believe, I cried for days. I had thought my biological father was John R. Lee. My brothers and I used to travel into Manhattan on the subway train to visit Uncle Buddy; and he used to take all of us to visit family members in Cleveland, Ohio where he would introduce us as 'his boys'. But, I never really thought about it...it just seemed like a term of affection. All I could wonder about the sound of his voice ringing in my ears was, *How COULD this happen?* I had so many mixed emotions and memories that kept playing over in my mind…. basically, it just blew me away.

Bob was my dad, but Lewis "Buddy" Cook was my biological father. We called him "Uncle Buddy". He was a big man, about 6'2" and weighed about 250 pounds. I am 6'2" and resemble him physically, with similar bone structures to his. Uncle Buddy had long black wavy hair; I wear my hair short, but it is almost the same texture. His skin tone was slightly darker than mine. Buddy, an African-American and Cherokee Indian, was a chef in the New York City Theatre District, where he cooked for and dined with a lot of theatrical people.

Before I was born, my mom and dad, along with my siblings Tommy, Ida, and Lianna had lived in Harlem, near my Uncle Buddy's sister who had befriended my mother. Dad was still working on the railroad and he was out of town a lot so my mom nurtured her friendship with Buddy's sister and, ultimately, with Buddy. For a short time, my mother and Buddy worked together in a Manhattan restaurant. When Buddy's sister and my mother found out about a new housing development with low affordable rents, they all packed their bags and moved out to Queensbridge Projects on the Queens side of the 59th Street Bridge, now called the Ed Koch Bridge, named after the late Mayor Ed Koch.

We lived in the Queensbridge Houses located in Long Island City in the western part of the New York City borough of Queens. Queensbridge Houses had opened in 1939. The 3,142-unit complex, owned by the New York City Housing Authority is the largest housing complex in North America. It is located between Vernon Boulevard (which runs along the East River) and 21st Street, immediately south of Ravenswood power plant. Queensbridge gets its name from the Queensboro (59th Street) Bridge, which is just south of the complex.

The elevators in our building only stopped at the first, third and fifth floors. We lived on the third floor, so whether or not the elevators were working, we had easy access. We all slept in bunk beds—the two girls shared the first bedroom and the five boys shared the second one. My mother and father shared the third bedroom. When you walked into the apartment, there was a little hallway and off to the right there was a storage space camouflaged by a curtain. *That was where our parents would hide our Christmas presents and other things they didn't think we would find.* After you walked down the little hallway and passed the storage space, we had the dining-kitchen area, then the living room, another hallway with a closet; then the bedrooms and bathroom, where Jeff, the neighborhood barber, used to cut our hair.

During the 1950s, the management changed the racial balance of Queensbridge by transferring all families with an income of more than $3,000 per year (a majority of whom were *White*) to middle-income housing projects, and replacing most of them with *African American* and *Latino* families. In addition to providing safe and sanitary housing to many low-income African American and Latino families, this policy also promulgated racial segregation in public housing.

There were some basic amenities in the Queensbridge complex, like a central shopping center, a nursery and six inner courtyards for play, all of which were included in the original building plans. During the 1950s and up through 1970 Queensbridge Park was called "River Park," after the East River that runs next to it. There was also a smaller park placed conveniently right under the 59th Street Bridge called "Baby Park". My family enjoyed all the amenities of the parks, but knowing the dangers of the environment; my parents imposed strict curfews on my siblings and me.

As a product of Queensbridge, I had many entities that shaped my life, pushing and pulling me in all directions. But, I wasn't a dreamer; I was a driver who led the way, wanting to be a positive example to my siblings.

Unlike most of my friends and neighbors in the Queensbridge projects, I was fortunate enough to have both a mother and a father living in the same household, although it was crazy at times. I was the fourth and middle child, one of five boys and two girls. We were a close-knit happy brood, sheltered from much of the world by our parents' love—my dad's wise words and stern hand, and my mother's great meals and infectious smile. I have many fond memories of sounds associated only to the projects, such as housing personnel knocking on doors while announcing "Housing," men delivering bleach water, going from floor to floor loudly belting out "Bleach water!" and the Milkman dropping off cases of milk bottles clinking against each other.

Life for us wasn't easy, although we were never made aware of the financial conditions or the hardships we may have been facing as a family. Our rent was always paid and our refrigerator was always full of food. Like most of my friends, I wore hand me downs and handed down my hand-me-downs, until they could no longer be mended.

There are many surprises in life, including family secrets that could be destructive or simply strengthen an entire family. You may have things in your family that hit you hard, but you still need to forge ahead and become the best you can be. My family seemed to endure, and I became determined to "Make The Grade". **When you get knocked down, just get up and keep moving forward**...there are a lot of hurdles in life...but there are a lot of heroes who get over those hurdles.

I'm named after my biggest hero, the man who I thought was my "real" father. John Robert Lee was the first one at the school during parent teacher day, always getting involved in all of my sports events. If I needed to talk to him about school, sports, sex, girls, or any other situations I might have found myself involved in, he always listened and advised me. He was always there looking out for the well-being of the entire family, no matter what the circumstances. He always made sure we had food on the table, clothes on our backs and money in our pockets—he would give us his last dime. To me, he was and always would be my "Dad".

When Uncle Buddy said he had something to tell us, *Wow*, I didn't realize how deep a blow that would be. I was pretty young, and I'm sure there was a lot of rebellion that stemmed from that rude awakening. So, I just broke down and cried because the man that was raising me was, in my eyes, my real father. After all, I carried his name. I am Bob Lee, *Jr.*

John Robert Lee was the person who took us to school and constantly stressed the importance of education. He also took us on long trips outside of the neighborhood so we could understand that there was a whole lot more in the world than what we were growing up in. The "concrete jungle", our community was a world where we would see drugs and alcohol on a daily basis, every time we stepped out the door. But to "Dad", there was a whole other world, another side of the coin. We remained in awe of the beauty of the landscape when he took us driving on those little winding country roads. We were so excited every time we saw the animals, and we couldn't wait to go again.

Once I learned the truth about my biological father, my relationship with my Dad never changed. He might have known that I found out, but everything between us stayed the same, except that I loved him even more. There was like an understanding, a bond between us. If I were my dad, I don't know if I could have handled the reality the way he did, but he loved all of us the same—he didn't waver in any way. Apparently, Dad had an understanding with my biological father, Buddy, because sometimes he got in the car with us and we would all go on a drive together.

We used to go visit my oldest brother who was away in upstate New York. He had been a troubled youth and was sent to a facility upstate at an early age, so we used to drive up to see him; this was like a ritual every Sunday. After he revealed the truth to us, Uncle Buddy was a consistent part of the family unit. Soon after, my brother Cliff surprised all of us when he brought both fathers together and said; "Boys, I've got something to tell you. I feel like I'm the luckiest person in the world; now we've got two fathers!" Both of them smiled about Cliff's comment.

My biological father, Lewis Cook, better known as "Buddy", was born in Columbia, South Carolina. Buddy's father, my grandfather, was from Winsboro, South Carolina in Fairfield County. We sometimes went down south to visit my grandfather on his farm, where I used to see him picking butter beans and assorted other vegetables and fruit that the family ate. If they wanted meat they would send a family member out to round up a couple of chickens or shoot a hog in the head; everything was home gown. Grandfather was 104-years-old, some say 106, when he died. To this day, I remain in touch with the Cooks and often attend the family reunions, where I see my father's sisters, all of whom are close to 100 years old. Recently, I went to look in the hall of records and learned that the Cook family had migrated all over the country. Buddy Cook passed away in the mid-1980s.

The elders say that MC Hammer is a cousin. When I spoke to him about it, and shared where we came from, and how we were kin, MC Hammer introduced me to his son and said, "Hey, this is your cousin." Then he invited me to the family reunions.

I started going to the Jacob Riis Community Center under the direction of Bob Minor, Bob Welch, Miss Armsfield, Lou Benson and Hank Carter. Hank Carter helped to discipline me in sports with basketball, boxing and volunteerism. With the guidance of that wonderful friend, role model and mentor, I began to make the grade.

In the mid-1960s, young Henry (Hank) Carter had no idea that God would lead him down a path of healing through fundraising. Growing up in the tough Queensbridge section of Queens, New York, Hank traded city life for jungle life, and was sent to Vietnam. In the army, he rose to Sergeant and was awarded a Bronze Star, Good Conduct Medal and other military honors. When his tour ended in 1968, Hank returned to his Queensbridge neighborhood and found that violence and drugs had ravaged it. I was twelve years old at the time, fighting for my life, trying to avoid the pitfalls that accompanied my surroundings.

Queensbridge had been built with three playschool rooms and a library. It also had a community center with an auditorium where shows were presented, a gymnasium with a wooden floor that doubled as a wooden-wheels roller skating rink. Activity rooms were downstairs, and a cafeteria was upstairs, where the playschool children ate their lunches. Some of the downstairs activities included: tap dancing, ballet, arts and crafts, singing, playing the recorder, pool, knock hockey and table tennis, as well as Girl Scout and Boy Scout meetings. There were also after-school programs and deejaying, which always sparked my interest. Senior citizens had their own room in the building. During the hot summer months, residents enjoyed concerts in the central shopping area up the hill. The Fresh Air Fund sent under-privileged youth out to the Peekskill Mountains to release them from the crime and grit plagued streets.

Queensbridge has historically proven to be a hotbed of hip-hop musical talent, including famed producer Marlon "Marley Marl" Williams, who was one of my DJ's while we were growing up in Queensbridge. I introduced him to Mr. Magic who started working with me at WBLS in New York. Marley is a friend and one of a long succession of acclaimed artists from "The Bridge", as we called it. The Bridge became one of the most prolific hip hop-producing neighborhoods in the country. Marley's Juice Crew collective, hugely influential in the 1980s, featured among its members Queensbridge rappers MC Shan, Roxanne Shanté, and Craig G, all noted names in their own right. Most notable of today's Queensbridge hip-hop artists is the well-acclaimed rapper Nas, who has, since the 1990s, frequently used his music and lyricism to reference Queensbridge and its hip hop history. Other noted artists associated with Queensbridge include Prodigy and Havoc of Mobb Deep. Also basketball champ Ron Artest came from Queensbridge; I used to box with his father who was very athletic.

My dad also kept me under his wing and when he could, he would take me to one of his many jobs. He was always on me about learning, education and preparation. He encouraged me to get involved with sports because he knew that could keep me busy and out of the streets. In 1970, through the Jacob Riis Community Center, Hank Carter started an organization, in his spare time, known as United Queens. The intent was to get kids involved in basketball and boxing, in order to get them off the streets and away from a life of crime, fighting, and drug dealers. That's when and where I met Hank. I was now a fourteen-year-old teenager, needing a new direction and ready to turn a corner. I joined the basketball and boxing teams and I was sparring all through high school. From time to time Mr. Carter took us out of state to compete; it was a good diversion, while living in the projects;

I remember one particular experience when I was about 15 or 16-years-old. I went to Boston with another organization that I had joined. We competed against the Roxbury YMCA team. I was so happy to be out of Queens—I was like a wild, crazy guy. We had won and everybody was so happy, after the game. All we had to celebrate with was a couple of cans of Colt 45 that someone had gotten at the store. A "brother" came into the room and someone said, "Hey man, what's up! Do you know where we can get some weed?" He went into the next room and came out with two big bags of weed, dumped it on the table and told us to gather around. He rolled a joint and we passed it around. The music was playing in the background and it sounded like someone had his or her finger on the record...it was dragging. I got dizzy, so I laid down and noticed that the people were running back and forth, seemingly in slow motion. They were all running around, laughing; and I was lying on the floor, thinking *I got to get up* and they were still rolling joints. I went back to lay down again, feeling like I was brain-damaged. I felt like that for about 2 days—needless to say, that was my first and last experience with marijuana.

I was so relieved to get back home to Mr. Carter. He had been reluctant to have me travel without him and he would have been extremely hurt and disappointed with me if he knew what had happened.

To my parents and me, Hank Carter was a Godsend. As I grew older, boxing became the sport I learned to love most, because it was a one-on-one sport. It was good for me because it gave me focus—I had to learn how to fight the right way.

Boxing had been known to give misguided young men second chances in life. Carter taught me how to discipline myself to do the things necessary that would help me become successful, and for a while, boxing had become my life...my passion. I was tall, fast and a hard-hitter; so I did well and soon became very proficient and determined to win. We fought for the Jacob Riis Center, the Police Athletic League and the Lost Battalion Hall in Queens.

I joined the Golden Gloves® and was strongly considering becoming a professional boxer. Many former Golden Gloves® amateur boxing champions have gone on to become outstanding boxers and role models in our country. The Golden Gloves® program has led the way in promoting amateur boxing in the United States and has produced the majority of competitors for America's boxing teams in the Pan-Am and Olympic games. Former Heavyweight Champion of the World, Joe Louis was a Golden Gloves Champion in 1934. Many other champions, including Muhammad Ali (1960); Sugar Ray Leonard (1973); "Marvelous" Marvin Hagler (1973); Michael Spinks (1974); Thomas "Hitman" Hearns (1977); Johnny Tapia (1984); Mike Tyson (1984); Evander Holyfield (1984); Oscar De La Hoya (1989); Jermain Taylor (1998 and 1999), five time Golden Glove Champ Mark Breland (1981), and my brother, Golden Glove Champ Cliff Lee (1975) all got their start in the Golden Gloves tournaments.

My trainer, Vic Zimmett, was wondering why I didn't use my left hook, but I compensated by using the right hand. I shouldn't have gone into the tournament that year because I had a dislocated shoulder, but I had told my trainer I was okay. I was supposed to win the championship, but didn't. I didn't win because I couldn't get it all together—I was physically hurt. The following year, my brother Cliff went in the tournament and won the Golden Gloves. Had I waited another year, Cliff and I would have been in the championships together. My brother Cliff was a great boxer who can pick a person apart with either hand.

I continued to box and became so good at what I was doing. I didn't think I had to train for it anymore, until one day, when my attitude changed forever. I learned one of the greatest lessons in life… that I had to prepare before I got there. .. something my dad had been telling me for years. But, I had become lax and on that particular day, which will remain embedded in my mind forever, I didn't train before I took to the boxing ring. When I saw my opponent, fear began to set in because he looked so polished. He looked sharp and professional…and I didn't know what he had. He came in already sweating and looked like he was well-disciplined. I thought, *Wow! I know what it takes to be disciplined, but I didn't train. I didn't run my five-miles a day. I didn't hit the heavy bag. I didn't spar; I didn't do what was necessary to win. When you want to win, you have to do the right thing…prepare before you get there…*

I began to beat myself up because a big part of this game was mental. That was an eye-opening day, so much that I still talk about it. I learned the greatest lesson of my life about how you should "PREPARE BEFORE YOU GET THERE". Sometimes there are situations in life when you won't be prepared, but knowing what I know now, you must definitely prepare before you get there.

My opponent stepped into the ring and we went toe to toe for the first and second rounds. The third round came up and I couldn't even lift my arms because I was so tired. I couldn't move my legs either. My opponent knew that I was tired, so he tried to knock me out. He decided to throw this big punch from Alaska or somewhere; it came in with a roar. I saw it coming and knew I couldn't do anything about it, so my mind decided to tell my body what to do, like it so often does.

Look Bob, the punch is coming, just get under that punch and throw a punch to his midsection; and he's going to drop his arms and then there's that window of opportunity, his chin will be right there. Then just turn your body back around into position with a solid left hook (Bam, see ya) and just throw your hands high in the air and wave them like you just don't care; the fight will be over.

But my body responded, *what! If I bend my legs I may not be able to get back up!* So now I'm fighting myself and I'm fighting the guy who's coming at me. The punch came in and hit me and I saw stars, I looked to see if I was on the canvas. I wasn't on the canvas, so I figured *I must be still standing.* I didn't know where I was for a second and I looked up again. I thought there were three people coming at me; so I kept throwing punches, and every now and then I would hit one of those three people, until they became one again.

I tell that story in one of my speeches when I talk to the kids at the many schools, community centers and community-based organizations. **If you know you have something important to do, don't become complacent; take care of your business and always "Prepare Before You Get There".**

Hank Carter was one of the hundreds of dedicated coaches, who unselfishly assisted young people in the development of personal character and athletic skills. In February 2013 a building to include the old North General Hospital on Madison Avenue and 122nd Street in Harlem, New York was renamed and dedicated to Hank Carter.

SEVEN WAYS TO KEEP
MOVING FORWARD

1. Life for us wasn't easy, although we were never made aware of the financial conditions or the hardships we may have been facing as a family.

2. I wasn't a Dreamer; I was a Driver who led the way, wanting to be a positive example to my siblings.

3. When you get knocked down, just get up and keep moving forward...there are a lot of hurdles in life... but there are a lot of heroes who get over those hurdles.

4. It was good for me because it gave me focus—I had to learn how to fight the right way.

5. Sometimes there are situations in life when you won't be prepared, but knowing what I know now, you must definitely prepare before you get there.

6. There was a whole lot more in the world than what we were growing up in.

7. Get kids involved in basketball and boxing, in order to get them off the streets and away from a life of crime, fighting, and drug dealers.

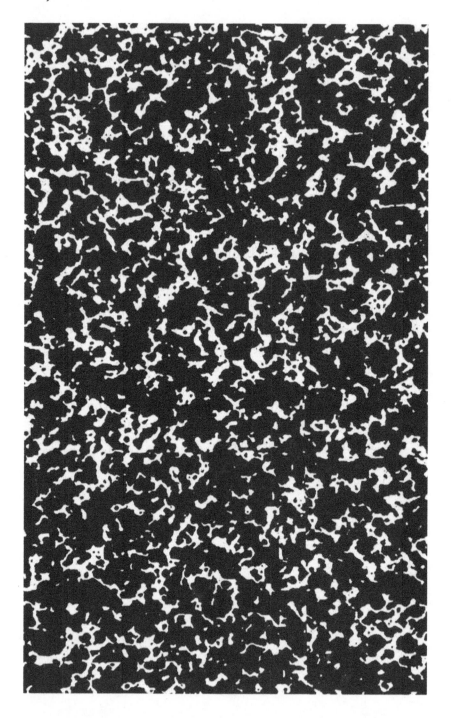

CHAPTER THREE

Becoming "Doctor" Bob Lee

*The whole secret of a successful life is to find out
what is one's destiny to do, and then do it.*
—*Henry Ford*

My dad, John Robert Lee needed to work a number of jobs; that's how he would make extra money to support our family. He was a doorman in Forest Hills, Queens off Queens Boulevard. There were several offices in the building and Dad would do extra work on the side to help out a dentist and a doctor. Every now and then, he took us to work with him. My sisters and brothers and I would clean the doctor's office and place things back where they belonged. The doctor had his long white coat hanging behind the door, so I used to put it on. He also had a big black powerful microscope. Sometimes my dad would let me play with it, while I pranced around the office wearing the doctor's coat.

Dad noticed my interest in the doctor's tools, so one Christmas he bought me a stethoscope and a microscope. Then, I started looking at all these microscopic organisms, like amoeba and paramecium, and even the microbes that I happened upon throughout the house. I loved chemistry and biology, especially now that I had been examining the little organisms as they were moving around, dying and splitting in two. It was not unusual to find me filling up a whole cabinet full of those little critters—stuff floating through the air we breathed—that most people can't see…but I could see everything. In fact, I was so enthralled by it all that, to this day, I can still envision those microscopic specimens. During that point in my life, I thought I wanted to become a doctor.

My interest peaked even more when my dad got me a chemistry set and I started mixing all kinds of concoctions. I made something one day, which was okay as long as it was contained in a heavy glass pickle jar. But I had spilled some of the mixture out on the ground and it started eating away at the concrete floor. I had no idea what I'd concocted and, after a while, I became a little nervous. I wondered how it could hold in the glass jar and why. But I never did figure it out; it was a mixture of everything I could find from the medicine cabinet and everything I could scavenge around the house. On one occasion, after learning the strength of my new discovery, I had a fight with the next-door neighbor. I thought, *all right, I'll handle this*. So, I poured some of the mixture on the concrete in front of his door and I waited and watched. The day I poured the concoction, I remember smoke started seeping under their door and there was steam inside their house. My neighbors got nervous because they thought there was a fire. *It probably cleared their sinuses and everything else*. From that day on, my neighbors always had a gap in front of their door and every time the porters would come wash the floor there was always a little puddle right in that gap.

That was the chemistry part of my life and that was when I earned my professional title. I was always working on something new and strange; and people would say, *all right 'doctor'*. Thus, *becoming* "Doctor" Bob Lee had nothing to do with music; I was mixing, but not mixing music…yet.

The way I got into broadcasting still has me chuckling. Unknowingly, my oldest sister, Ida, started me out on a career path that would become my life's passion. We used to have a Victrola and my sister Ida had a bunch of records with her initials on them. I used to watch how she put all the records together—the 45s. She would show me how to put the little yellow, green or red disk in the middle. I was about ten at the time. After the community center basketball games, while my parents were out working, Ida would have parties at the apartment. I would crawl out from my bedroom into the living room, along with my brothers and sister, and we would watch her and her guests. Ida always used to catch me, though, when someone would say 'hey your brother is alongside the couch'. Somehow, my brothers and sister always got away without being caught; but she would beat my butt and put me back to bed.

One day when my mother came home, I told on Ida and she got in trouble. I said, "Mommy, she had a party...everyone from the community center was in the house dancing." My mother told Ida that she couldn't have any more parties; but she continued to have the parties anyway, and I kept coming out to see them. One night when Ida was having a party, she called me out to the living room and said, "Alright Bobby, here's what we're going to do. Do you want to play the music?" I said, "Yeah, let me play the music." Ida told me, "I'm going to let you play the music; but you're not going to say a word to mom and dad. I told her 'okay'. She said, "Put the red disks in this stack of records; they are the fast-tempo records. The green disks are for the mid-tempo and the yellow disks are for the slow-jams."

I began to learn how to put the mid music and up-tempo music together with the slow ones. I would use those little disks to separate the records and I used to stack them up. People did the two-step, the jerk and the boogaloo, and I would deejay from the furniture, dropping one record at a time. People waited for me to drop those grinding up, red light, basement party slow jams. You didn't have to mix in those days and people always knew what to do between the records. They usually walked off and got a drink and then came back to the dance floor.

I kept playing and getting better; and by the time I was fifteen, people started hiring me to play for their house parties. Ida bought me my own record-player, complete with speakers and I would get 20 or 25 dollars to play. I had my black doctor's bag, so I put my records in there with the things I needed to clean them off, along with all the disks and a variety of different color light bulbs to set the atmosphere...and I always brought my stethoscope...keepin' it real. It was my first real business.

Those were some interesting years, when I was deejaying on those old Victrolas that people had in their homes. *You had to lift up the top and it had an automatic turntable inside.* That's what I used when I started deejaying back in the day.

On one occasion, my friend, Michael Lewis, and I decided to go outside and play at a block party. The people came outside and danced. We didn't have the proper DJ gear yet, all we had was a turntable, a receiver and a lot of little speakers. The DJ's who were more advanced saw what we had and how we mixed and they started laughing at us.

They rolled out their Shure speaker on a dolly hooked up to a car battery and a cassette. They blew us away and took over the party. They were the ones playing regularly out in the community, so we learned from them. The looks on their faces and those laughs forced us to spend a lot of money, to keep from being embarrassed again. We weren't playing the community center events yet because we were still trying to get our equipment together; but when we went to the community center and saw the possibilities, our entrepreneurial spirit kicked in.

The light bulbs went off in our heads and we came up with a great plan. We were finishing up at the house parties, and when the people left the room, we looked at the records and copied all the names and addresses of the record companies. Then, we would go to the record companies; we said that we were mobile DJ's and wanted to play their music. We would go home with all the records before anyone else had them and we played all the hits, or what we thought were hits, or what would become hits, at our parties. Whenever we played in our little room at the community center, the people left the crowded room where the other deejays were and came to our room to rock with us. We were the new kids on the block, the talk of the hood. They wondered where and how we got the latest records that we played before anyone even heard them on the radio. We threw our hands up in the air and yelled. *We were The SUPER SOUNDS DJ's and on our way!*

A few years later, when rap emerged as the newest trend in our community, I wrote a rap for Frankie Crocker who was on WBLS-radio in the seventies. Frankie Crocker, a veteran radio broadcaster and program director, helped catapult WBLS-FM, the black-music format radio station, to the number one spot among listeners ages 18 to 34 in New York City. On the air, he sometimes called himself the Chief Rocker, and he was as well known for his self-aggrandizing on-air patter as for his off-air flamboyance. He wore his hair long and drove flashy cars. He had the best of everything…clubs, music, women. When Studio 54 was at the height of its popularity, Mr. Crocker rode in through the front entrance on a white horse.

Frankie thought my rap was a poem and he announced, "This kid from Queens, Bobby Lee, sent me a poem! I'm going to read it to you when I come out of the commercial break!" Frankie read it as a poem. It was about WBLS and that was the first rap on the radio. *Who would have believed that years later this kid from Queens named 'Bobby Lee' would be one of WBLS' top on-air personalities and the station's Community Affairs Director working with the Steve Harvey Morning Show, receiving numerous awards for the "Daily Dose" from the American Association of Broadcasters?*

While attending Junior High School 125 in Woodside Queens. New York, my childhood friend, Angel Fontanez, got me interested in the printing business. I took the exam to make it into the New York School for Printing, which later changed its name to the School for Graphic Arts and Communications. Because I enjoyed what I was doing, after graduating from high school, I decided not to go into college right away. Instead, I got, what I considered, a great job in the printing business, where I worked for about a year and a half as the night foreman. I operated a long web fed press with about eight ink and varnishing stations. The chemistry was to have the ink dry well before it got to the take up reel, otherwise plates would get twisted and you would have ink everywhere. I found a way to run the press so fast that my work was done by the time everyone came in the next morning. I used chemistry to help make the ink's varnish dry faster than normal; it was a secret I held for a while before sharing the process with some friends in the business.

During that same time, my family moved out of the projects and purchased a house in Jamaica Queens, where I occupied the basement and set up a music studio. I had many interests and income streams, doing pretty well financially, and I was keeping very busy. While I was working at my printing job, I was still boxing and thinking about turning pro. I was also modeling professionally and in addition, playing my music. *I've always had any kind of music you would want.* I continuously upgraded and kept a great-sounding sound system because people were always hiring me to play private parties...to this day.

Playing basketball and football were still part of my life, but they weren't standing out among the most important things. Later on, I realized that I had to make a choice and narrow my focus. *You need to pinpoint exactly what you want to do because if you do that,*

God will give you all the things necessary to help you become successful in your chosen field.

My focus was wide because I was doing so many things. I was thoroughly enjoying my life; then the music bug took over and all my other interests subsided. On weekends, my crew and I loaded up the van with the best sound and lights. We began to tour colleges and universities. My friend, Angel was part of the crew. He used to perform at our junior high school talent shows as the drummer from the band Young Gifted & Ready. When he performed, I was his roadie. *I used to carry all of the drum equipment and set him up for the shows. I would have enjoyed being part of the band, participating as a musician, as a bass player.*

One particular weekend, while on tour at Howard, Adelphi and Farmingdale Universities, my crew and I traveled to Upstate New York to Oswego State University. It began to snow that Friday night, which turned into a wicked storm. We were right off of Lake Ontario; the wind and snow were blowing so hard they had to put up ropes around the campus to keep people from blowing around. We were snowed in. I wondered if it would clear in time for me to get back to work on Monday because my boss was tough and we had a big printing order in for the week.

At the time, Angel was dating a girl named Zulaka Abdul whom, coincidentally, I used to like in the 3rd grade. Zulaka and I used to write love notes on pieces of paper, fold them up and pass them back and forth. During the Friday night party at Oswego, Zulaka introduced me to a beautiful, smart young lady named Jackie Wiggins who was in her junior year at Oswego State University. The crew thought Jackie was cute. She would wink, and then do this thing with her finger, where she would point and motion you to come over to her. Jackie and I danced and began to talk. She asked me where I lived and I said, "I represent Queens." She then told me that she was raised in Brooklyn. After a nice long conversation, Jackie said, "You have a nice voice, did you ever think about going to school for it?" I told her 'No'. She asked if I had ever been to a radio station before. I said, "No, but I listen to WWRL & WBLS in New York." She said that she would show me the university's radio station in the morning. I responded with little interest, "Oh, okay."

After the party, we looked outdoors and realized that nobody was going anywhere. Angel from the crew had set up the sleeping arrangements in the girls' dorm. We all looked at him as if he was crazy; but then again he was always full of surprises. That night was one of the best times of my life. I had the opportunity to visit a real radio station… and I was in love. It was a blessing that our paths had crossed. I will always be grateful to Jackie Wiggins for her foresight, friendship and advice.

After I got back home from the college tour, I returned to my job at the printing place and my boss came in fussing that I had missed a lot of work. I told him that I couldn't make it back due to the storm; and by the way, I found my true love and I'm going back to school for communications. He said, "Communications, my ass! Get your ass in there and finish that job!" But I was determined to change my path and I left. He was fussing at me all the way to the car and told me that I wouldn't amount to anything.

So I decided to enroll in a college close to home. My choice was the New York Institute of Technology next to Columbus Circle in Manhattan. They had a radio station called 88.7 WTNY, where I became a jock, then music director, program director and, in my senior year, general manager.

In the summer of my junior year we got the crew together and loaded the van with the sound system and prepared to take a trip to Columbia, South Carolina to visit the Southern part of my family. We all stayed at my father Buddy's house on the same property with my grandfather. When we arrived, my cousin Rusty told us that a big club by the name of the Electric Warehouse needed a D J. and sound. We were at the right place, at the right time. We went in to meet the owner and he had us working that very night. It was a massive place with stores in it, a huge dance floor, and a big stage with massive lighting on it… waiting just for us. The owner of the club had connections to the radio stations, the Big DM 101.3, WOIC and a few others, later owned by Inner City Broadcasting Holdings. The owner set us up to broadcast from the lobby of the club, where we would watch the dust kick up in the parking lot as cars drove in from all over.

We were a big hit, like rock stars, talking on different radio stations and listening to our voices on the radio with commercial spots: *Doctor Bob Lee & Company from NYC Live at the ELECTRIC WAREHOUSE each and every night.* We used to mix the music…they never heard that before… and radio stations never played it like that. Program directors and record company people began to fill the VIP section and would-be rappers showed up to hear us rap. The Electric Warehouse was packed seven nights a week as we rocked the hell out of it. There was no shortage of people, especially girls, waiting to *talk* to us at the end of each night. We rocked the House and the radio station, the Big DM, until my Dad said *get your butt back here to New York to finish school.* He never stopped pushing me about the importance of education.

We packed up and while we were at the loading docks, loading the van with our sound equipment, one of the club managers watched over us. After we hung our outfits into the van (clothes for deejaying—doctor uniforms) preparing to head home, the manager crawled into the back of the van and snatched the outfits out and held them, as if for ransom. Walt Sweet from the crew said, "Wait a minute, I left something in my pocket "and the manager held the uniforms up. Walt grabbed it and ripped the pocket. The manager whipped out a gun, pointed it and yelled with a deep southern drawl, "I never did like you niggers anyway!" I yelled out, "Put that gun away! If you want the outfits take them, but the club bought them for us!"

Racism! Another great lesson learned—everything was fine as long as they were making money off our backs; but when the money stopped, racism reared its ugly head. But, boy, did we have one of the greatest experiences of our lives! The crew—my brothers, cousins and friends are still talking about it today.

During my senior year at the New York Institute of Technology I started applying for jobs and internships at radio and TV stations. Many responded, but only Fox Five, WBLS and 1600 WWRL piqued my interest. Hal Jackson, then VP of WBLS, Inner City Broadcasting responded, "Well, we have no jobs, but we'll keep you in our files." So I wrote to Hal again and said, "How about an internship?" And he said, "We have an internship program. Do you want to start in March?" I told everybody, "Hey I have a job!" *I knew it was only an internship.* I agreed to work for free and then I learned what the job was all about. I used to do all the deejay work for Frankie Crocker, who years before had read my rap on the radio as a poem, and whom I had admired since I was a teenager.

After my internship ended at WBLS-Radio, my friend Bert Lewis, who I had worked with in South Carolina, had gotten me a job at WOKB where he was the program director in Tampa Florida; but WBLS called me in and said they wanted to hire me. They said, *we have a van and we want you to go around to different places, so whatever you come up with, let us know.* I always wanted to get into the school system, and here was an opportunity to work with the community. I was doing freelance, at the time, getting paid $100 for an appearance. As my popularity grew, I was doing 3 to 5 appearances a day and by the end of the year, Charles Warfield—the General Manager of WBLS called me into his office and said, *Hold up, wait a minute.* After a while they put me on payroll because I was making too much money, at the time, for *appearances.*

That's when Ken Webb and I came up with the "WBLS On Time Program". We visited schools throughout the Tri-State area (New York, New Jersey and Connecticut) trying to encourage students to stay in school and be on time for class.

Ken Webb was on the air during that time—he worked the shift indoors from 6-10 A.M.; I worked the shift outdoors from 6—10 A.M. We would put different schools on the radio and when we pulled up at these schools the students would be waiting for us in full force—sometimes there were as many as 2000 people outside. We used to broadcast from the telephone booth. Frankie Crocker always gave us a bag of change to feed into the phone and I knew where all the working telephones were. One morning, I went to Kennedy High School in the Bronx and we pulled up in front of the school, which was about a half a block away from the telephone booth. We invited all the kids down to the telephone booth and Ken Webb was in the middle of broadcasting an 'on air' contest. He told me, *Hold on Bob; let me do this contest and I'll be right back.* So all the kids came up close to the van and I had the side door open so they could hear the radio station.

And then Ken said, *Let's go back to Bob Lee! Bob what's going on?* And the kids all yelled, *Yeah!* Ken Webb finally came back to us and all the kids were out there on the sidewalk. It was packed; I had thousands of students in front of me singing Whitney Houston's "The Greatest Love of all" along with Whitney on the airwaves. Then Ken Webb would lower the music and just let the thousands of kids in front of the high school sing. Whitney knew what was going on with her music and called to thank me.

It was so loud. Ken said, "Bob can you hear me!" I said, "Hey we're out here live in the snow!" On Time and in full force at Kennedy High School in the Bronx! Hi! What's your name and what do you want to do when you graduate? We figured that usually when someone tells 3 ½ to 4 million people on the radio what they want to do, that they would follow through, so this was a good incentive. We were in the middle of talking to the kids and the operator popped in and said, *please deposit 10 cents for the next 5 minutes or your call will be interrupted. Thank you, this is a recording.* The kids fell out in the snow, laughing. I was stuck with the phone in my hand. Then Ken Webb said, *"Well I guess the operator had to get her 10 cents worth."*

We had a good time that morning and that was the start of something new. When we got back to the radio station the Chairman, Percy Sutton, said *I would like to see you in my office, Bob.* And I said, "Aw shucks, what did we do?" Mr. Sutton called in one of the engineers in and they opened up a briefcase and in the briefcase was a cell phone. I said, "A cell phone!" And Mr. Sutton said, *Yeah! You can make phone calls from the van! From now on, you can plug this into the lighter and you'll be good to go…*

As "Doctor" Bob Lee, I have been blessed to become one of the most recognized entertainment personalities in New York. My career in radio, music and television spans over 30 years. I began in 1979. Then in 1981 I earned my BA; later I earned my MA in Communications from New York Institute of Technology, where I was a DJ for 88.7 WTNY Radio. I later advanced to Music Director, Program Director and eventually General Manager of WTNY Radio. In 1980, I joined WBLS for a one-year internship before moving on to 98.7 KISS-FM for my start in commercial broadcasting. Thereafter, I returned to WBLS where I have had a rich and diverse career. *Years later, unbeknownst to me, the two stations would merge and I would be back full circle.*

From 1986 to 1994, I was a DJ on the weekend edition of WBLS's renowned program "The Quiet Storm" and have for several years provided live reports on the morning show from various WBLS-sponsored community events. I have interviewed such musical greats as Stevie Wonder, Patti LaBelle, Luther Vandross, Jaheim, Mariah Carey, Mary J. Blige, Kenny "Baby Face" Edmonds, Biggie Smalls, the O'Jays, Wynton Marsalis, Bobby Brown, Whitney Houston, P. Diddy, Jill Scott and Beyonce', among many others. I can now be heard on air every day with my award-winning "Daily Dose" series, tackling health issues, which affect the community.

In addition to my on-air roles, I am also the Community Affairs Director for WBLS. As part of my community-based work, I have developed strong ties to many local and national politicians and public figures, including President Bill Clinton, Mayor Michael Bloomberg, Mayor David Dinkins, and Bronx Borough President Ruben Diaz Jr. I also currently host the weekly live television program "Open," which broadcasts on Bronx Net, a cable television station serving the Bronx and upper Manhattan. The program features news and topics affecting our community and also treats viewers to new and established musical guests.

I appear frequently on all the summer stage concerts throughout the five boroughs as the host of live music productions and other events, such as Harlem Summer Stage and R&B concerts at the Apollo Theater. In addition, my strong ties to the community are reflected in my many charitable endeavors. Among other activities, I am a founder, President and CEO and a board member of the *Make the Grade Foundation,* a not-for-profit organization that provides mentoring and aid to school children. I also help college students interested in radio careers by serving as a mentor for college radio stations and I am involved in corporate speaking and promotional work for businesses with an interest in the welfare of the community.

I say this, If you stick with something long enough, something always happens...but make sure it's positive. Follow your dreams. Find out what you want to do in life and you, too, will Make the Grade.

Seven Ways to Find Your Purpose

1. I was always working on something new and strange; and people would say, *all right 'doctor'*.
2. I kept playing and getting better; and by the time I was fifteen, people started hiring me to play for their house parties.
3. When we went to the community center and saw the possibilities, our entrepreneurial spirit kicked in.
4. *. You need to pinpoint exactly what you want to do because if you do that, God will give you all the things necessary to help you become successful in your chosen field.*
5. I agreed to work for free and then I learned what the job was all about.
6. I have been blessed to become one of the most recognized entertainment personalities in New York.
7. My Dad said *get your butt back here to New York to finish school.* He never stopped pushing me about the importance of education.

CHAPTER FOUR

What's It All About!

Education is the most powerful weapon,
which you can use to change the world.
—Nelson Mandela

Make the Grade Foundation is the collaboration between the parent, teacher, student, community, and clergy, with the health component and financial literacy in the mix. We discuss all those things that are useful to help youngsters become successful by guiding them in the right direction. I am personally giving back, trying to help the kids do things the way they used to be done—by showing them the care and concern that I experienced from my parents, teachers, community, and clergy when I was growing up. It is of great concern to me that, even when it comes to something like playing simple games like jacks, checkers and other board games, or dodge ball, hide and go seek, or jump rope, they don't experience the same quality of games that we used to play. There is very little interaction or physical challenge because everything is so technical and only requires thumb coordination. Youth today spend a lot of time alone and thus there is very little comradeship, teamwork, bonding or loyalty.

Although games are important to round out your personality, Make the Grade Foundation stresses the education factor first and foremost by offering a series of programs. By being well-educated, our youth will not have any guarantees, but they will at least become a more confident and more competitive person in the job market when the time comes for them to step out on their own.

Remember the fight I mentioned in Chapter 2? I won the fight because I had won the first two rounds but it was the worst fight I ever had experienced. However, it taught me a great lesson. Today when I talk to the students, I tell them to "prepare before you get there". If you know you have something coming up, something in class, a spelling bee or anything, you've got to go over and over it until you get it right. Then when it's time to take the test, you will win.

Make the Grade Foundation members, staff and volunteers from the corporate and local communities gifted with the ability to connect with young people regularly visit schools, and make presentations focused on encouraging academic progress and commitment to excellence. Make the Grade Foundation offers six specific programs that address the well-being of the participants.

The Cool 2B Smart Program was part of our curriculum for several years. When we were doing this program, Make the Grade focused on increasing classroom attendance in schools, by having competitions that improved math and reading skills. This motivated students to attend and participate fully in the educational process, while employing positive peer pressure.

Through Academic Enrichment Programs Make the Grade Foundation arranges educational fairs to inform students, parents, teachers, and school administrators of existing programs and organizations in their communities, partnering with programs/organizations such as: Score, KUMON, and Sylvan Learning Center.

The College Preparatory Program partners with organizations and arranges college tours, fairs, and informational sessions and raises awareness about collegiate opportunities, college choice and college life.

The Mentoring—Tutoring Program partners with school guidance counselors, teachers and parents. The program identifies students in need of role models and one-on-one help with academic subjects. *Mentors also assist in securing summer jobs and internships/apprenticeships for mentees with interests or skills in particular areas.*

Through the College Scholarship Program Make the Grade Foundation's long-term goal is to raise funds to provide annual monetary college scholarships to students who have shown significant academic commitment, progress, or growth in high school and community involvement.

The Partnering with Parents Program organizes informational seminars and fairs for parents and families, addressing various topics critical to maintaining physical and mental health within families, e.g. the importance of nutrition and eating a healthy breakfast before school, obesity, coping with asthma, diabetes, depression, peer pressure and conquering learning disabilities.

The Make the Grade Foundation, along with its sponsors, is responsible for building Internet Radio and TV stations for community-based organizations—schools, churches and community centers and hospitals. This is a great way to teach the students how to sell themselves, present themselves and how to communicate well. *How do we do this?* We utilize radio and television strategies using professionals from the media. We have workshops. We bring the students on tour to radio and TV stations, show them how the clock works, what commercials are all about, how important timing and mathematics are, while presenting their overall message.

We also show the students that radio, television and the media have a major influence on the lives of the people in our community—often controlling the way people think. It's a fact that you get your heredity from your parents; but, realistically, the biggest controllers of the people—the most influential ways and means to move the crowd—are the media, which include propaganda, education and religion.

In addition to the normal programs of Make the Grade Foundation—I have a Make the Grade Foundation Shadow Program. We host up to 30 students, including elementary to Junior High, on up to college students, usually in their Freshman or Sophomore year. On the average, their ages may range from 15 to 20 years old and it consists of a wide range of young people, who are seeking career placement in the broadcasting and communications industry.

With the Shadow Program, I take college students because they're looking to get out into the job market and they're seeking out internships and entry-level positions. So we bring them into the radio station (WBLS) and we show them what the different jobs are all about. Even if they're in their freshman year or sophomore year, sometimes after coming up to the station, some students change their curriculum and decide to get involved in broadcasting. I usually like to be there for all of the students and be hands-on when they come into the station, but sometimes when I can't be there, we are fortunate to have other mentors participate in that day's program.

By conducting these visits and tours of the radio station, we are able to let the students know that the people they hear on the radio or on the microphone are not the only ones involved in the broadcast business. There are a lot of people behind the scenes who help make this happen; so we introduce the students to those people and we show them other jobs and alternate positions that might pique their interest.

You have to know how to present yourself and communicate in society. If radio or TV is not what they want to do, it's still beneficial. There's social politics that some governments of the world use to control its people and the media: radio, TV, magazines, newspapers, Internet, religion, and the department of education. The left and the right, the democrats and the republicans fight to gain control of the media, education and religion. Whoever can control those entities can get people elected.

Although working with college students is very rewarding, I also like to go to elementary and junior high schools. The younger students are still malleable; you can really get into their minds and teach them. I find that, once they get into high school, you can still teach them, but their minds are made up and they are pretty much set in their ways through peer pressure or through just being a part of the whole system. By growing up in their communities, the young people have often been pre-conditioned into becoming the person they are going to become; but it's never too late to change. The high school kids of today are a little more modern in their thinking than when I was growing up.

It's most ideal for Make the Grade Foundation to start with the younger kids—we have a lot of very intelligent young people out there who started reading in preschool. When children are in preschool, I go to them and speak about education and treat them like the intelligent youngsters they are becoming. I even go to nursery schools, and the children and I really get into it. I sing right along with the kids, songs like "If You're Happy and You Know It, Clap Your Hands"; "The Wheels on the Bus Go Round and Round" and

"Old MacDonald Had a Farm". Then I get the children to sing their ABCs and they understand that this is the foundation for whatever they will be learning as they grow older.

While partnering with Affinity Health Plan, partners, students and parents, we would usually ask for the very young kids. We talk about nursery rhymes and ABCs and I ask them, "Do you like to read?" I always get a resounding, "Yeah!" Then I tell the kids, "If you like to read, we want you to read up to 12 books during your vacation, and when you come back we'll give you gift certificates for Toys R Us!" And the kids say, "Yeah!" Once the kids are all fired up and excited about reading the books, the teachers take charge and they let the parents know that Make the Grade and Affinity have this reading program.

During their summer break, some of the children read 12 or more books that are sanctioned by the school. In order to qualify for the gift certificates, they have to fill out a Q & A. Of course, the type of books they read are not very thick, so they are not challenged too much by the assignment. When they head home, we give them a questionnaire and when they return, we can tell if they have read the books based on the five questions we ask. For example, we might say something like, "What's the book about? What did you think about the big bad wolf?" Depending on the answers, we'll know if the children have actually read the books.

The parents are usually helping out their children, as well. The teachers contact the parents and when we come back in September the teachers have figured out who actually read what books. We come in to the school and bring a number of $50 gift certificates, which we'll give to the children who have read 12 or more books. A lot of children in the audience who didn't read their allotted books during the summer are now encouraged to read them when we come back the next time.

Affinity Health Plan sponsored the Summer Reading program and their company purchases the $50 gift certificates for the children. Affinity Health Plan is a non-profit managed care company that provides health care services for over 200,000 low and moderate income residents around the New York City area. Since its beginning in 1986 as the Bronx Health Plan, the Affinity Health Plan's dedication to improving the public sector has set a standard for the development of the State Medicaid care program and subsidized programs for the uninsured. The Make the Grade Foundation has been fortunate to have the Affinity Health Plan as a program sponsor since we launched in 2004.

During the thirty years that I've been doing this type of community outreach, I have made at least one appearance at almost every school in the tri-state area (New York, New Jersey and Connecticut). In a single calendar year, of course, we cannot do a program in every school, but we look for the schools that need it the most—like those in the most troubled areas and other criteria like that. We also have a follow up on most of the schools that we adopt, which I feel is very important.

Through the years, our outreach has been handled in different ways, depending on the logistics of the school and the time allocated to us. We make our selections in a number of different ways. Many of the people we've had relationships with over the years stay in touch with us—those teachers, principals, and superintendents still contact one another. And then, there's word of mouth. Those same teachers may tell other new teachers and then we get letters from them. I may say something about Make the Grade Foundation on the radio and then the teachers may email or call me and leave a phone message. The principals, teachers and parent-teacher leaders, or presidents or guidance counselors give us a call personally. We also work with the Department of Education (formerly the Board of Education) and are sponsored by The United Federation of Teachers. UFT is comprised of individual principals and teachers and different organizations or corporations; the president of UFT is Michael Mulgrew (the president of UFT). New prospects are also often selected from someone else who may be working with the Department of Education.

Make the Grade Foundation does not deal with parents on a one-on-one basis. When the schools have their parent-teacher meetings we try to encourage the parents to attend by coming up with different incentives, but unfortunately a lot of parents do not show up, regardless. That's something we're trying to improve upon, so we create incentives. We ask the parents to come, get involved and have dinner, or we give away movie tickets or tickets to a play. If we can get the parents to attend the meetings, then we have the opportunity to get a message through to them and let them know how important it is to share in their child's education. Because of our incentives, a lot of parents do show up but there is a larger percentage of parents who do not; and many of the students don't want their parents there, anyway. We understand that parents are busy, but they must get more involved with the education of our children. It's okay with them in elementary school and in parts of junior high, but as the students get older, especially when it comes to high school students, they think it's sort of embarrassing to have their parents at the school.

The "it's uncool to have your parents around" syndrome actually starts in middle school. Then it continues from age twelve and above. The older the kids get, the more difficult it becomes to mold them because they are so much more vulnerable to the peer pressures and dangers present in our society. Much of the breakdown with their parents occurs when these 'tweens and teens begin to lose respect for their parents and the kids begin to rely on their peers for all the answers, right or wrong. Peer pressure may or may not lead the way to their detriment, but because of it, far too many young men and women are ending up in the clutches of the law, incarcerated, addicted to drugs, or dead. Make the Grade Foundation is constantly waging the war between the good and evil of society in an attempt to steer our youth in the right direction, uphill to success. It leaves a lot of weight on the successful delivery of our messages.

The adolescent stage is very tough—it's a tough part of growing up because many of the kids feel sort of in the dark. You don't want your parents around—you want to show that you're a man or a woman—but you're not yet a man or woman. Young people also operate impulsively, emphasizing the magical thinking "syndrome—it can't happen to me, I'm too slick," all of which is inconsistent with their brain chemistry—making parental/adult guidance all the more important and relevant.

You're an adolescent, you're not there yet, and you still need that parental guidance; but a lot of you don't want to accept adult direction because there's something else whispering in your ear or texting you—peer pressure, your boyfriend, your girlfriend, your so-called friends, and maybe even your gang members. You probably think that everybody you come in contact with in your age range is "it" because you believe everyone knows what's going on. And anybody's opinion, older or younger than you doesn't really matter. You probably think, *He's too young, he doesn't know what's going on;* or if your older brother or sister gives you advice, you might think, *He or she is too old.* So there's that generation gap that these kids have to deal with, but they don't like to deal with. They want things right away—*give it to me now, give it to me now*—instant gratification, without putting in all the work necessary to make it all happen.

Recently, I've even come to realize that from about 8-years-old, you become more and more influenced by the world. For some Middle School kids—twelve years old—it may already be too late to mold them. So, lately, we always tell these younger kids, "It's important, if you're going to hang out with a group of people, make sure you guys are all leaders, and make sure everybody knows right from wrong. It's important that you are a leader and you're not following anybody." Then we say to these young kids, "How many people here have brothers and sisters and nephews and nieces and cousins and friends and little people in their lives?" Usually everyone in the auditorium will raise their hands and I say, "Guess what! Those little people— your little brothers and sisters—you can get them hurt because they are trying to do what you do and they are looking up to you, and if you're not doing the right thing, the can get hurt. So make sure you're always doing the right thing. You're the leader, so don't follow anybody because you know right from wrong. Do you not?" And the kids all respond, "Yes we do!" They're looking up to you to guide them in the right direction.

For Make the Grade Foundation, "leadership" can drive home the most positive influence for kids who are age eight and up. They come out of that protective shell of being under mom and dad and the family and they start to get more open to what's going on in the world. Their minds are beginning to get more and more developed in that area. Before that, they're all up under their mom, very heavily dependent on their parents, and then they start hanging out with their friends, good and bad. At this point, it's up to the parents to make sure they are in God's hands.

When it comes to audience participation, if we fully want the kids to engage, we have open discussions in the classrooms. I've personally sat in an auditorium and watched the interaction, which wasn't always pleasant. But, based on our experience, if you have a smaller controlled group, you're right there up front in their face. The students won't open up in the auditorium, so whenever possible, if the classroom sizes are smaller with about ten people, this is the best option for close-up intervention, as opposed to an auditorium. It really touches on the emotions when the kids are able to open up in these small groups. You can conduct a discussion in an auditorium if you want, but if the kids' friends are present, they'll probably be laughing and joking. Then, they'll usually look at their friends before they give their answer, which may or may not be factual. In the smaller environment, they will have no excuse because they won't have to worry about what the next person thinks; so they'll come out, and talk and share more.

To get small groups, the criteria are that you set it up with a teacher. I say to the teachers, "Give me the most vulnerable students, the ones you think are most troublesome. Let me talk to them for a while." And I let them know that I don't want to talk to them just one time because that doesn't do anything—I always want to follow up. This also lets them know you care about what they have to share and that by participating they might be more apt to finding a solution to whatever challenges they are experiencing. At this point, these students become more confident that they may have a chance to Make the Grade by being acknowledged as part of a special "family" or group.

SEVEN WAYS TO STAY ON TRACK

1. Youth today spend a lot of alone time and thus there is very little comradeship, teamwork, bonding or loyalty.

2. By being well-educated, our youth will not have any guarantees, but they will at least become a more confident and more competitive person in the job market when the time comes for them to step out on their own.

3. If you know you have something coming up, something in class, a spelling bee or anything, you've got to go over and over it until you get it right.

4. The younger students are still malleable; you can really get into their minds and teach them.

5. Much of the breakdown with their parents occurs when these 'tweens and teens begin to lose respect for them and the kids begin to rely on their peers for all the answers, right or wrong.

6. The adolescent stage is very tough—it's a tough part of growing up because many of the kids feel sort of in the dark.

7. It's important, if you're going to hang out with a group of people, make sure you guys are all leaders, and make sure everybody knows right from wrong.

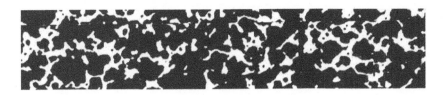

PART TWO

The Seven Steps

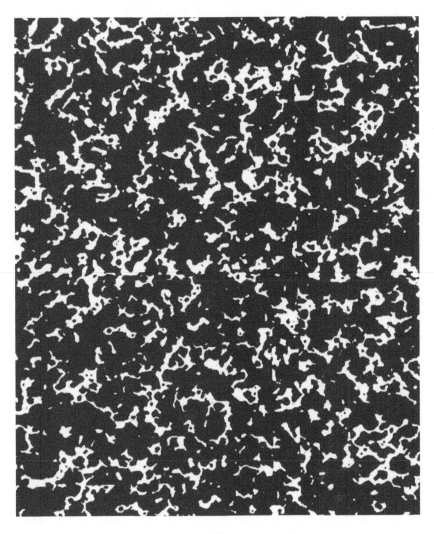

ONE
The Parent

Your children need your presence more than your presents.
—Jesse Jackson

Instead of just dropping your kid off to school and treating school like it is a babysitting service, I think the parent needs to get together and sit side by side with that kid to help him or her with their homework. The parent should go to the school and find out what's going on, make friends with the teacher, keep in contact with the guidance counselor and principal and get to know whom you need to know and everything that's going on in school. Volunteer—make yourself visible. As a parent, also know whom your kids are hanging out with. That's very, very important.

When my dad told me, "You can have all of this if you stay in school, study hard and stay out of trouble," he always said it in a loving manner. As I look back on those childhood days, I realize how important it was for him to repeat that message over and over so that my brothers and sisters and I could have a bright future. He knew that it only took one mistake to destroy our lives.

When your children are in the adolescent stage, don't just throw your hands in the air and give up when they start acting up. In a lot of cases, when kids start becoming rebellious, don't forget that you have probably gone through some of the same experiences at their age. Try to understand that they are going through adolescence into adulthood, and just encourage them. Don't give up because they may not rebound, and as long as you give them that needed foundation, they will probably straighten themselves out, and grow through that wild time.

As they mature, your children will eventually understand what you went through when they were teenagers. As long as you give them that foundation, they may even come back one day to thank you. When I learned that Uncle Buddy was my birth father, I acted out and did things that I regretted, but my dad understood and stood by me through it all. He made sure that I would grow out of it by offering his love, support and wisdom—thus I was able to become a successful young man, who would Make the Grade for myself and help many other people do the same.

I learned early that it was good to follow my instincts and become a leader, but one time I got caught doing something innocent and harmless...or so I thought. One day, my friend Eddie and I were walking down the street and we passed by an abandoned car. After thinking about it for an instant, we went back and got into the car and pretended like we were driving. We were in our own little world, dreaming about country roads and high-speed adventures. Before we knew it, a police van pulled up and the officer made us get out of the car. He handcuffed us and ordered us to get in the back of his police van. We wondered what was happening to us because, after all, we were just sitting there playing with the car. We were about seven or eight years old, at the time, so you can imagine how terrified we were. We didn't have any seatbelts on; so we were bouncing around all over the police van, while being driven down to the police station. When we arrived, the officer called our parents—that was a very frightening day. Although it was an innocent mistake, it did not go unpunished. I really caught it from my parents when I got home.

When I think back, I realize how fortunate I was to have three parents, who really cared about my well-being, especially knowing what so many young boys and girls are going through, with absolutely no mother or father-figure to rely upon for advice, companionship or concern.

My biological father, Uncle Buddy, probably influenced me subconsciously, in some ways, but he wasn't big on education and neither was my mother. But they were always there when I achieved academically by graduating and for other major achievements in my life. My "Dad" was big on education; not a day would go by without hearing him say, "Stay in school. Be on time." When he came home from work, he sat at the table reading; he would always have a book, an encyclopedia or a newspaper open in front of him. *I get the chills thinking about those images of daddy.* My younger brother, Tony, was usually sitting in Dad's lap and he taught us all to read well, at an early age. We always sat around the table with Dad reading together.

We had all of the volumes of the World Book Encyclopedia, and every year we got a new one when the encyclopedia man knocked on the door. They were a world of information. The encyclopedia was published in the United States and self-described as "the number-one selling print encyclopedia in the world." It was designed to cover major areas of knowledge, but showed particular strength in scientific, technical, and medical subjects. I'm sure that's why it piqued my interest. I was so excited every time a new edition arrived. I learned that the first edition, which was published way back in 1917, contained eight volumes. New editions have since appeared almost every year since its first publication. In 1960, twenty volumes were published; dad first introduced the World Book Encyclopedia to our family in the early 70's. We really enjoyed reading them... the words were spelled out really big and they had beautiful illustrations. A few years later, we started to receive National Geographic every month; after I got a job, I subscribed to the National Geographic and began sending it to my dad.

My Dad left home at a young age. He tells a story of being at an age where he was about to graduate from high school. He was supposed to be tending to the garden, but instead he was talking to a girl over the fence. His dad came from behind him and hit him on the back with a hoe. This caused him to run away from home, not graduating from high school. He had to take care of himself and work instead of going to school, so he became self-educated. Because he was deprived of a proper education he always said that he wanted us to have more, to know more, and to be well-educated.

Hal Jackson, who broke me in as an intern at the radio station reminded me a lot of my father. He also left home as a child, had similar mannerisms to Dad, and was the same type of caring person.

Hal Jackson was orphaned at the age of eight, and like my father, he was out on his own at the age of thirteen. Hal didn't let a whole lot bother him, but when he got upset, you'd better look out.

You might say I was born and bred in the projects; it was the place I called home since my birth.

Right after I entered the world, I went home to the projects with my parents and was greeted by my two older sisters and a brother. Dad had so many mouths to feed and because of his commitment to educate us, it had been literally impossible for him to save enough money for a down payment on a home. But, after my Dad received a settlement from a car accident, he purchased a home.

You never know where your blessings will come from; sometimes they happen so fast, and you've got to be ready. So when my family finally had the opportunity to flee the concrete jungle, it was truly deemed a blessing.

My Dad had gotten into an accident on his way to visit my brother Cliff and me at a place called Children's Village, which was located in Dobbs Ferry, New York. When the public schools were being desegregated, we had been labeled as "juveniles", taken out of the public school system and sent away to a boarding school. There were a number of cabins on the campus and we had house parents who would temporarily act in the role of our regular parents—like foster parents. Every now and then we would go home for the weekend; but every week when we didn't go home Dad visited us there. Sometimes he came with my mother, sisters and brothers, or just by himself. We were at Children's Village for two years.

One particular day, Dad was very tired from working long hours. Cliff and I were sitting on a rock in front of the office, waiting for Dad but he never came. We were beginning to get worried and I said, "Wow what happened?" Then we got a call from the office. They told us that while my Dad was driving, there was an accident. My two youngest brothers—Tony and Eddie—were riding with him. They were all taken to the hospital, where they remained for quite a while. One of my brothers, Tony, hit the dash and fractured his skull. My father hit the steering wheel and broke his arm. Eddie, who was in the back seat, was traumatized. When my dad had the accident I was about 10-years-old.

My mother diligently saved the money from the settlement and several years later we had enough money for the down payment on a house. My family could finally move out of the projects. I was about nineteen-years-old.

When our family moved, we left a lot of memories behind, some good, some not so good. Most of all, amidst all the changes, the friendships, the dangers, the injuries and the growing pains—my parents showed my brothers, my sisters and me so much love and concern. Without the comfort of the most caring parents in the world, I often wonder, *Where would I be now?*

I left my parents' home and moved out on my own when I was about 22. For three years, I had been dwelling in the basement, where I had set up my own little apartment, complete with a music studio.

I have tried to model myself after my dad, my namesake John Robert Lee. I often think about Dad's wonderful qualities, his relationship with his children, and what a wonderful role model he was, not only to his children, but to all those young people he encountered throughout the years. Vivian and I have three children and five grandchildren who are all doing well. My son Shiheim is an educator; he has two daughters: Anisa and Siona, and one son, Shayne. My oldest daughter Shekire, who just scored the highest GPA in her class, received her nursing degree, supported by the G.I. bill. She recently received an honorable discharge from the United States Navy. Shekire has two children: a son, Jonathan and a daughter, Natalia. My youngest daughter, Sheena, who is a recording artist, sings gospel music. She has recently released her first album on iTunes. "Destiny" by Sheenah Lee features Bishop Hezekiah Walker. As parents, we should continue to stress the importance of love, family and education.

I have often reflected about my childhood. As I realized my blessings, I became determined to reach back to help those children and offer a helping hand to those who are striving to achieve. That's why I founded Make the Grade Foundation.

There are far too many kids who are cheated out of the experience of living in a two-parent home. And, yet, there are many who do have that experience but they may be living in a loveless household filled with abuse, lack of resources and addiction. I have run across just about every situation: childhood prostitution, pregnancies and kids who are really hungry because their parents are taking drugs instead of buying food. These kids have to talk to somebody in the schools, community and church to get them the help they need.

The Police Department has a youth program, too. So, if the kids have a problem that needs special attention, the police refer them to an organization that can handle it. Parents, I know how it is trying to talk to some kids these days. If you see something, say something; hand a youngster a note as to where they may get help.

Make the Grade Foundation also has people on the board of directors who are connected in those areas. Our board members are working people who get involved within the program, utilizing their expertise in various fields. We have working board members and advisory board members. I also have a vice president, Denise Rogers. Together, we do a lot of the hands-on interaction, and we have volunteers who like to do hands on, as well. Those who are too busy work on the phones. I always urge the kids to give me a call, whenever they need to talk to someone. I am one of several voices that they hear on the phone.

Role Models Who Have Made the Grade

Debrah Harris-Johnson is a mother of two and a professional mediator who focuses her energy on helping youth make the transition to adulthood a little easier. In her book, **The African American Teenage Guide to Personal Growth, Health, Safety, Sex and Survival**, Debrah said this about the relationships between teens and their parents:

> *Healthy and constructive parent-child interactions (should) lead to warm and loving relationships. This, in turn, promotes the development of happier, more confident, and more secure children. In short, mutually rewarding family relationships are*

not just accidents. They are the result of positive interactions between parents and their children. However, the reverse is also true. Repeated parent-child interactions filled with scolding, tension, accusations, and unpredictable emotional outbursts can strain even the best of relationships…most parents don't want to seem cruel or inhuman…they should instead take a moment or two to think about how much their children mean to them and how good their child can make them feel…they make you laugh; they make you proud…they care what you think, what you say, what you do, and how you are feeling. They love you, trust you and miss you when you are gone. They probably come to you for just about everything…it's gratifying to be loved and needed like that. It's great to be a parent!

On the other hand, because many parents today are facing numerous problems stemming from unemployment, housing, imprisonment, drugs, abuse and more, many young people experience stress at an early age. Thus an unhealthy relationship results and often causes irreparable damage to your child's life. A key problem area in the unhealthy relationship (between parent and child) involves antisocial behavior.

According to Ms. Harris-Johnson:

By antisocial behavior, we don't mean shyness or poor manners. What we're talking about here includes a variety of high-intensity behaviors performed at the expense of others or their property. Fire-setting, theft, and extreme cruelty are common examples of anti-social behavior. The repeated use of "hard" drugs and/or alcohol also falls into this category. Anti-social behavior is extreme, as well as dangerous. If you notice that your child is beginning to behave in this fashion, staying out very late at night or all night long, get some professional help right away. The longer you wait, the greater the chances are that someone will get hurt. And if that happens, you and your child may well find yourselves up to your ears in legal problems.

A number of different family structures exist today. Among the many structures: there are teens whose mother and father live together, or whose mother and father live apart, or who have only one parent, or whose parent or parents have adopted them, or who live with a parent and a stepparent, or who live with an aunt, an uncle, grandparents, a grandmother, a grandfather or other relative, or who have same sex parents, or foster parents. Many of these variables, particularly those that are non-traditional, may contribute to societal controversies and future relationship adversities.

One day you are going to have to make intelligent decisions if you are on your own. Make decisions based on the substance of the matter. You can't blame it on your parents and your circumstances. Regardless, continue to make intelligent decisions. There comes a time in life when we all have to make intelligent decisions about finding our purpose in life. We may have a combination of different family structures in our life, like me. I found out my Uncle was really my father. Sooner or later we have to utilize and realize that all of the things we have encountered in our lives have made us whom we are. It's up to you to choose…right from wrong…success or failure.

Clara Hale was one of the most well-known and adored "foster parents" in New York City. And although her direct impact was felt locally, her influence spread far and wide. She received more than 375 awards and 15 honorary degrees in her lifetime.

Mrs. Hale's remarkable legacy of caring for children started over 70 years ago, when at the age of 33, she became a widow and was left to raise three children on her own. She started caring for other children in her home in order to make a living that could provide a home and education for her own family.

After providing day care and respite care services, Mrs. Hale became a licensed foster parent in 1960 and took even more children into her home. It was during this time that she earned the affectionate title, "Mother Hale". Mrs. Hale took in seven or eight children at a time. Eventually she reared 40 foster children, keeping them out of trouble and steering them from the temptations and dangers of the street. Mother Hale emphasized reading, good behavior, and above all, honesty. All the Hale House children made it through high school and many went to college.

◇◇◇

Regardless of the family structure you are raising your children in; it is up to you as a parent or "foster" parent to keep your children safe from harm. Always find time to listen to your children, no matter what their age, so they have the best possible chance of growing up as upstanding and responsible citizens. And remember, honesty is the best policy. If you are facing problems, find a way to share them with your children and let them know they can always share their problems with you—no matter how small or how big they are. Being honest can save a life.

For a few years, when I went to boarding school, I had cottage parents; but I turned myself around and made it out in good standing. Discovering that my uncle was really my father, coupled with the desegregation thing, made me very upset. The school administration felt we (black kids) were coming into their domains and going to damage their neighborhoods. They weren't giving us the necessary attention, academically or otherwise, so they had their social workers and guidance counselors call our parents, and instead, sent us to neighborhood programs. Then, they started recommending places like Children's Village. Today, you hear some of the parents talking about how the school system diagnoses kids with having ADD (Attention Deficit Disability) and gives them drugs like Ritalin, which becomes a stigma on the kids' records.

It is so important for parents to assume the responsibility for their children. But, that is not always possible, given the ills of our society and the climate of most inner-city communities. When children are not being cared for properly or being abused, their life and the lives of those around them could be in danger. Acting like an adult does not always fall into the hands of grown people; sometimes young people must step up and report wrong-doings to those in authority. We must all make a commitment to protect our youth through outreach and concern, whenever the need arises.

Asadah Kirkland, mother of one child, but considered mother to many, has been working with children for over fifteen years. Her work with young people has involved teaching and working diligently to solve problems within their families.

The award-winning author's first published book, *Beat Black Kids* is designed to encourage better actions amongst her parental peers and should help parents make better decisions for the greater good. According to Ms. Kirkland:

> *A child's contribution to the world does not have to come hard. Struggle does not have to be involved. There is nothing wrong with things being easier for them. Easier feels good and has great value if we have the skill as adults to create it.*

> *Our children will populate the world in the future, as adults. There is no denying that. What kind of adults will they be is the question. As parents, we influence the answer. Will we put them in a corner or give them the opportunity to decide on something? Will they remember our beatings or will they remember our wisdom?*

The key, as parents, is to continue to give our youngsters all the tools necessary to help them become successful. That includes taking them on trips, giving them classes, interacting with their teachers, attending their extracurricular activities, and more. With all these incentives in place parents and guardians will certainly help their children to Make the Grade.

SEVEN WAYS TO
BECOME A BETTER PARENT

1. *As a parent, also know whom your kids are hanging out with.*
2. "You can have all of this if you stay in school, study hard and stay out of trouble," Dad always said it in a loving manner.
3. When your children are in the adolescent stage, don't just throw your hands in the air and give up when they start acting up.
4. You never know where your blessings will come from; sometimes they happen so fast, and you've got to be ready.
5. There are far too many kids who are cheated out of the experience of living in a two-parent home.
6. We must all make a commitment to protect our youth through outreach and concern, whenever the need arises.
7. Always find time to listen to your children, no matter what their age, so they have the best possible chance of growing up as upstanding and responsible citizens.

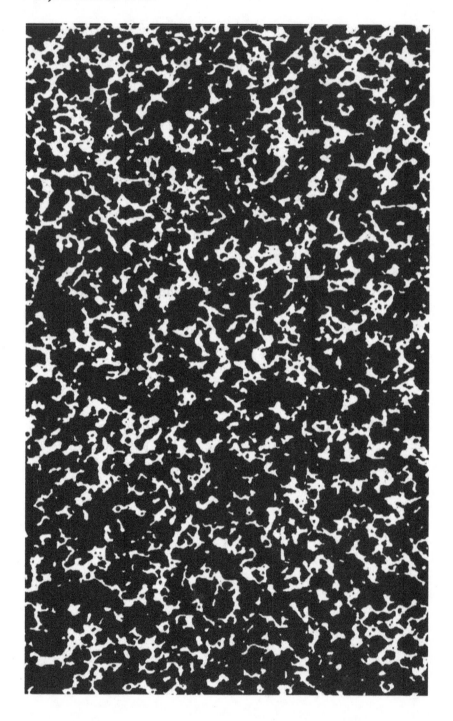

TWO
The Teacher

The dream begins with a teacher who believes in you, who tugs and pushes and leads you to the next plateau, sometimes poking you with a sharp stick called "truth.

—Dan Rather

Make the Grade Foundation works very closely with the teachers' component, starting with those teachers who educate pre-school children right up to those who steer our young adults through college. Some teachers come to work just to make a paycheck, but there are others who are very very passionate about teaching and educating our youngsters. They are truly sincere about educating these young minds, and that's extremely important. Some teachers will stay after school, some will start after school programs, and some will give out their home or cellphone number for students to call. The teachers know which students want to excel because they will ask questions and say, "Hey, I'm having trouble with this," and they'll help the students out with that or at least they'll try to. The teacher is very important to the future success of our youth.

In my early school years—kindergarten, first grade, and second grade—we had really nice teachers. The school was right in the neighborhood about three or four miles from home. That was great, but then the racism kicked in. I was about 8 years old and in the third grade when my brother, Cliff, and I were bussed to another neighborhood. The teachers in the new school were upset and we wondered why. They never came over to us when we raised our hand and they ignored us throughout the day. There were only one or two people of color in our classrooms and the teachers wouldn't teach any of us. Eventually the guidance counselor would speak to us and if she couldn't help, there was a social worker who got involved.

We didn't have a learning problem; the problem was that we were not getting the attention everyone else was getting. So, the protocol was to send us to the guidance counselor. If you weren't up to par, the social worker would contact your parents and recommend you to an alternative school. *As I think back, it was the system's way of ignoring desegregation and keeping segregation alive.* The mission was to get you into a type of *reform* school that the school system had set up. They apparently had their ways of doing things that would racially divide the communities and keep African American kids from progressing.

My brother, Cliff, and I were removed from the public school situation for two years and we went to Children's Village, a private (boarding) school, which was based on a 277-acre farm in Dobbs Ferry, New York. It was designed to create a home-like environment with cottages grouped in neighborhoods and a central quad for academics, work and recreation.

Our parents and a social worker conferred and decided to get us out of public school because the teachers were not teaching us. That was also around the time when they started medicating kids, saying they had attention deficit hyperactivity disorders and things like that, so I imagine everyone involved thought it would be best to change our environment.

The primary goal of the Children's Village clinical program was to help children improve their emotional health, to raise their self-esteem, and to help them put behind the problems and issues that have become barriers to their happiness and success. Maybe the teacher's intervention was a good thing, but at the time, I felt even more hurt and dejected. Through it all, though, my Dad never missed a weekend without either visiting Cliff and me, or bringing us home. It must have been very difficult for him, between going upstate to the facility to see my older brother and then shuttling back and forth to the Children's Village on the weekends and working all week.

In Junior High and High School, my interests began to spike in a variety of ways. Between the biology, the chemistry, the music and the sports, I stayed very busy. Fortunately, my junior high school teachers noticed that I had special interests and the talent to go with it and they led me to the School of Graphic Arts and Communications in New York City. I had to take a test to get in; it was first called the New York School of Printing.

After high school I studied Communications at the New York Institute of Technology, where I earned both my Bachelors and Masters Degrees. Currently, I am pursuing my PhD at The American Institute of Holistic Theology. I am majoring in The Philosophy of Metaphysics Dealing with Natural Healings.

It was exhilarating to hear President Obama speak at a recent National Action Network event hosted by Reverend Al Sharpton. He topped off his speech by speaking about education, citing that, *"Every child deserves the right to a good education."*

"If we want to attract new jobs and new opportunities to our shores, we've got to make sure America can out-compete the rest of the world. It means we're investing in cutting-edge research and technology like clean energy—and most of all, making sure we are giving every one of our children the best possible education. The best possible education is the single most important factor in determining whether they succeed. But it's also what will determine whether we succeed. It's the key to opportunity. It is the civil rights issue of our time."

President Obama also said, *"When there is an achievement gap between students of different races and backgrounds, that's not a Democratic problem, that's not a Republican problem—that is an American problem that we have to address. When too many of our schools are failing our children, too many of our kids are dropping out of school, that's not a black or white or brown problem—that is an American problem. We're going to have to solve that problem. We are all responsible for the education of all of our children. That starts with parents making sure that we're doing right at home, staying engaged in our child's education, and setting high expectations. Without parental responsibility, nothing else we do will matter. But we also know that each of us has a responsibility not just as parents, but also as civic leaders, as Americans, to do a better job of educating our children."*

"We're going to have to take the same approach when it comes to fixing No Child Left Behind. Instead of measuring students based on whether they're above or below some arbitrary test, we need to make sure our students are graduating from high school ready for a career, ready for college. That's what we need to do. Instead of labelling our schools a failure one day and then throwing up our hands and walking away, we've got to refocus on the schools that need help the most. In the 21st Century, it's not enough to just leave no child behind. We've got to help every child get ahead. That's our goal—get every child on a path to academic excellence. And we need to make sure that that path leads to a college degree."

"The only way for America to prosper is for all Americans to prosper. We've seen that in the census that just came out. The face of America is changing. You can't get away with having a third of our children, half of our children, not doing well. Not today, not in the 21st century. All of us—black, white, Latino, Native American, Asian American, men, women, disabled, and others—in America, we rise and fall together."

It was obvious to me that President Obama, too, had experienced some racial bias as a child and he wants to make sure that these acts of prejudice stop, particularly toward innocent school children who just want to learn.

My Dad had always stressed, "Stay in School." So I did. I studied hard, I got my degrees and I am still not finished. Not only am I continuing my education; but my children are too. We meet many great teachers along the way, who are caring and concerned with giving their students the structure to reach their fullest potential. Every now and then, we will come across one who doesn't help his or her students strive, so we move on and we learn what it takes to Make the Grade.

I always tell students that in order to get the most out of their relationship with the teacher, they should have a few considerations:

○ Pay attention and listen to what is being taught. Even if they don't want to speak-up and get involved in classroom discussions they should always take notes and be aware of everything that is happening around them.

○ Be aware that they can't fool their teacher. Teachers always figure out whether or not students are studying. If they do not have their assignment completed, they should say so and be willing to accept the consequences without a fuss.

○ At the least, students should attempt to do their assignments; they will be acknowledged for at least trying. Teachers are professionals, so if there are personal or family problems that students have shared with them, this will be taken into consideration. The teacher might even offer help before students ask for it.

○ I also stress that students should be courteous to their teachers; they should not whisper or pass notes to other students during class and never talk back to their teachers.

I believe that a teacher can and should do more than just teach. A teacher's responsibility is to help the students. They should be unbiased and never judge a student by his or her *physical* appearance. However, if there is reason to be concerned, the teacher should address that concern first with the student, then with the parents and the guidance counselor—not necessarily in that order. Although a teacher doesn't always offer to help, it is up to the student to at least ask; otherwise they will not know that you actually want or need their help.

Ms. Marva Collins is probably the country's most recognized teacher who went above and beyond her assumed responsibilities to educate her students. She has received many accolades in recognition of her outstanding work with children. When asked about her student success ratio, Ms. Collins stated: "Don't try to fix the students, fix ourselves first. The good teacher makes the poor student good and the good student superior. When our students fail, we, as teachers, too, have failed."

Marva Collins grew up in Atmore, Alabama at a time when segregation was the rule. Black people were not permitted to use the public library, and Marva's schools had few books, and no indoor plumbing. Nonetheless, Marva's family instilled in her an awareness of the family's historical excellence and helped develop her strong desire for learning, achievement and independence. After graduating from Clark College in Atlanta, Georgia, she taught school in Alabama for two years. She then moved to Chicago and taught in Chicago's public school system for fourteen years.

Marva's experiences in the Chicago school system, coupled with her dissatisfaction with the quality of education that her two youngest children were receiving in prestigious private schools, convinced her that children deserved better than what was passing for acceptable education. That conviction led to Marva's decision to open her own school on the second floor of her home. She took the $5,000 balance in her school pension fund and began her educational program with an enrollment of her own two children and four neighborhood youngsters.

Thus, Westside Preparatory School was founded in 1975 in Garfield Park, a Chicago inner-city area. During the first year, Marva took in learning disabled, problem children and even one child who had been labeled by Chicago public school authorities as borderline retarded. At the end of the first year, every child scored at least five grades higher proving that the previous labels placed on these children were misguided. That little girl who had been labeled as borderline retarded, graduated in 1976 from college Summa Cum Laude. Marva's graduates have entered some of the nation's finest colleges and universities, such as Harvard, Yale, and Stanford, to mention just a few. Many of them have become physicians, lawyers, engineers and educators.

I believe that our teachers are sheroes and heroes who have been put on this earth to carry out one of the most important missions that any woman or man can undertake; and I recognize that *a truly special teacher is very wise, and sees tomorrow in every child's eyes.*

Because of the dedication and commitment of the thousands of teachers throughout the country, our youth have an opportunity to build a meaningful future. Education, however, is but one component that goes into Make the Grade Foundation's commitment to give our youth the best possible platform for their successful future.

SEVEN WAYS TO EXCEL AS A TEACHER

1. *Some teachers come to work just to make a paycheck, but there are others who are very passionate about teaching and educating our youngsters.*
2. I recognize that *a truly special teacher is very wise, and sees tomorrow in every child's eyes.*
3. *The teacher is very important to the future success of our youth.*
4. We meet many great teachers along the way, who are caring and concerned with giving their students the structure to reach their fullest potential.
5. My junior high school teachers noticed that I had special interests and the talent.
6. If there is reason to be concerned, the teacher should address that concern first with the student, then with the parents and the guidance counselor
7. The good teacher makes the poor student good and the good student superior.

THREE

The Student

We have an obligation and a responsibility to be investing in our students and our schools. We must make sure that people, who have the grades, the desire and the will, but not the money, can still get the best education possible.

—Barack Obama

Our goal is to help students make the grade and do all the things they need to become successful. We tell them they must step up to the plate and not just stay in one place and think everything will come to them.

At Make the Grade Foundation, we teach kids to identify their purpose. I go to them and explain, "Look, when I was your age, sitting at home like you, I didn't know exactly what I wanted to do. But it's okay if you don't know right now, because you will eventually identify something in your life, something that you love doing. It could be your hobby. You don't want to be working on something and not love it, so make sure you get involved in something that you really enjoy doing because you're going to have to work for most of your life, until you retire. When they first started paying me, I told them, *you've got to be kidding me, because I used to do this for free.* I said *you guys are paying me for what I really love doing? I love this!*"

Sometimes, your focus is so wide that you don't know exactly what to do. When you begin to narrow down that focus, it shows. Here's a personal illustration: when I used to box, I also played football and I participated in other sports. I deejayed and got involved in music; I even learned about and got involved in the printing business.

But it wasn't until I narrowed it all down that I began to flourish in the one or two things that I really loved doing.

If you pinpoint something that you're really passionate about, God will give you thousands of ideas to help support that. You may come up with ideas that are out of this world, possibly some new inventions, because God is backing you up and giving you the knowledge to complete the task. It sounds like an easy plan—focus and invest—but even professional athletes and famous entertainers have to practice many hours in solitude to make their jobs look "easy." They create a mindset of self-discipline to match their passion. That's what successful people do. So stay on the straight and narrow, study hard, set your goal, and go for it. You may encounter a few pitfalls along the way, but don't let that discourage you; your determination can keep you on course.

God must have had plans for me, because there were times when pitfalls caused me more than discouragement. Many of my encounters involved bullying incidents—peer abuse—that stemmed from aggressive behavior from older students or people my age who didn't place much value on someone else's life. This may occur at school, church, family activities, the workplace, home and in your neighborhood; and it may exist between social groups and social classes. I had two specific encounters with bullies who could have put an end to my life's journey. As bullies often do get away with their actions, both did, and both went unpunished.

I was a tall thin kid who came from a not-so-great neighborhood and I was bi-racial, which was not very common in my immediate community, especially during that era. Those circumstances may have been the cause of some of the incidents that I encountered, but I would one day become more confident about whom I was and whom I could become.

My first encounter happened when I was just 8 years old. In the summertime, there's often too much idle time and a lack of constructive activities. The kids have the fire pumps open getting sprayed to keep cool. They had it on full blast so it was very powerful. I was standing there watching the action, thinking that I was pretty far away. Suddenly one of the older kids lifted me up, held me over the water spray for a moment, and then let me go. The last thing I saw was my feet in the air. Then I went airborne.

The water carried me across the street into an oncoming car. I hit the car and ended up underneath it. I had been run over and was lying under the car, with the water rising up around me. I was drowning. I could see the front wheel of the car. I put my arm around that wheel and pulled myself out from underneath it. The water kept pushing me back up underneath the car. I managed to climb out of there, having nearly drowned. I was banged up and run over, but somehow I got up and started walking. Water was in my eyes and everything was blurry. I wiped my head; blood was all over my hand and dripping down my legs. My friend looked at me and said, "Oh, shit!" I realized at that moment that I was severely injured. As I think back, I find it amazing that the driver left the scene, the police never showed up, and the kid who did it had run all the way down to St. Rita's church to hide, about six blocks away. They found him kneeling in the pews; he thought I was dead. The miracle was—I was actually walking home.

It must have been a little less than a quarter mile to get home. Along the way, people who saw me said, "I told you that you shouldn't have been playing next to that pump!" I felt some stinging on my back, so I raised my shirt and asked my friend what he saw. I said, "Is there anything on my back?" From the look on his face, I knew it wasn't good. He repeated, "Oh, shit!" I had a big gash alongside my spine. We lived on the third floor and I had to walk up the stairs because the elevator was out of service. When I came to the door, I found out that my father was home. *Thank God!* Every now and then Dad came home for lunch. My mother saw me first and yelled "Oh, no!" My father quickly moved the chairs out of the way and put me on the floor. My mother yelled, "Bob!" Dad put a towel around my waist and around my head to stop the bleeding. I was soaking wet from the fire hydrant, so I didn't realize how much blood I was losing. I had lost a lot of blood—fast! Dad picked me up and rushed to the car. He put more towels on the car seats and ran through the traffic lights to get to the hospital quickly.

I stayed in the hospital about two weeks. I was almost a goner. I still can't believe that I walked home; it was a miracle. I had been drowning in my own blood. Thank God, the car that hit me stopped after he heard the thud, but he didn't take me home. The kid that did it actually walked away; his family said they didn't have any money, so he got away with it.

I may have done little mischievous things, maybe some crazy things, but I was never a bully. It was so obvious what the consequences of bullying could bring. Maybe to the other kid it was a prank, all in fun; but if I had died, he might still be in prison, or worse.

Years later, I had another close call when we got into a nasty car wreck. I was about 20 years old and still living life on the edge. Dad was in the back seat taking a nap and I was driving his car. After visiting Dad's family, we were in Chicago on the Indiana Turnpike. They had given us sandwiches to take with us and I was eating one of them. I had it in my left hand, while driving with my right hand on the steering wheel. It was raining really hard. I was just cruising and I noticed headlights coming up on my right side, then they went in back of us and came up on the side again. I thought, *What the heck is going on?* The third time the car passed us on the right side; then it must have gone out of control. It was beside our car and I was doing about 70 miles per hour. I hit the brakes to avoid hitting the other car and it made our car hydroplane. We started spinning around and all I saw was spiraling lights all over the place. We were completely out of control, going 70 mph on the highway.

My father woke up suddenly and he was out of control too. He wasn't able to grab the steering wheel or put his foot on the brake, or the gas, or anything. He was holding onto the back seat screaming, "Son of a bitch!" We had totally lost control as we went down an embankment and ended up next to a farm. We climbed out of the car just as the young lady's car came barreling down behind ours. She jumped out and was standing there in the rain, dripping wet. I'll never forget how she looked; she was a young white woman, probably in her late teens, with long brown hair, yelling at the top of her lungs, "Is everybody all right?" We all just stood around in a daze. I was on the hood of the car. When we looked around, we realized that we had stopped right before the guardrail. There were skid marks all the way down from the highway. We had been dangerously close to tumbling down to the road below.

Driving to endanger can be considered another form of bullying. A lot of kids die each year as a result of drag racing, driving too aggressively, speeding, or just breaking traffic rules. Although we were strangers prior to the accident, because of the aggressive way this particular young woman was driving, I relate to it as bullying.

The incidents stated above are examples of actions related to bullying. Sometimes it's just words, but more often it goes far beyond a verbal altercation or teasing. When you are young, you are tempted to do and say things 'just because'. It could be just because someone dares you, or just because you don't like someone, or just because you want to show off. Whatever the reason, teasing or bullying, or just because, can often lead to the serious injury or even the death of your victim. And, just because you didn't think about the consequences of your actions, you could end up doing life in prison or getting the death penalty. *Life's mistakes are made in seconds…it's how you fail!*

Bullying is a common tactic directed to kids who may be part of a social group that is considered "different". One such social group that is steadily increasing is the number of mixed-race children being born. According to Census data, the population of mixed-race kids in the U.S. has soared from approximately 500,000 in 1970 to more than 6.8 million in 2000. Research on these kids has highlighted some of their difficulties:

- ❖ The disapproval they faced from neighbors and members of their extended families

- ❖ The sense that they weren't "full" members in any racial community

- ❖ The insecurity and self-loathing that often resulted from feeling marginalized on all sides.

It's very likely that, as a bi-racial child, Barack Obama had insecurities, particularly when confronted by his peers with the tormenting question "what are you?" Barack has parental roots in two countries (United States and Kenya) as many of our young people have today. Based on our society's norms, it would seem apparent that as a young student Barack would have been teased, taunted or bullied by his peers. Such a "forced-choice dilemma" often compels children to claim some kind of identity — even if only a half-identity — in return for social acceptance. Not all children can accept such a challenge and many times their schoolwork suffers first.

Barack was born in Hawaii on August 4, 1961. His father, also called Barack Obama, was a college student from Kogelo, a village in western Kenya, a country in Africa. His mother, Stanley Ann Dunham, was from Fort Leavenworth, Kansas. They met when they were both students at the University of Hawaii. His parents divorced in 1964, and his mother and maternal grandparents raised Barack. In 1967, Barack's mother married Lolo Soetoro, and moved the family to Indonesia. His half-sister, Maya Soetoro, was born on August 15, 1970. In 1971, Barack moved back to Hawaii to go to school, living with his grandparents. That year, Barack's father visited him in Hawaii; he would never see his father again.

Many of our youth face similar challenges of being raised, not by their parents, but by their grandparents instead, creating a generation gap and an almost certain communication gap. Some find that it's a difficult adjustment and the imminent peer pressure to flaunt youthful parents often surfaces; thus, another level of bullying from fellow students might occur.

Instead of dwelling on what could have been negative aspects of his life and feeling sorry for himself; Barack obviously used any negative energy to aspire. Many kids grow up in similar circumstances and have excuses or reasons why they can't achieve in school, but Barack apparently took his challenges head on. He was a good student, not necessarily a "model student", but he always aspired to be better.

After graduating high school in 1979, Barack attended Occidental College in Los Angeles, California. After two years, he transferred to Columbia University (in New York, New York), graduating in 1983 with a bachelor's degree in Political Science. His father had died the previous year (1982) in a car accident in Nairobi, Kenya.

In 1985, Barack moved to Chicago, Illinois, and worked as a community organizer, helping people improve their lives and become voters. In 1987, he travelled to Kenya, visiting his father's hometown and meeting many of his relatives.

The next year, 1988, Barack enrolled at Harvard Law School in Cambridge, Massachusetts. In 1990 he was elected the first

African-American president of the Harvard Law Review (a very prestigious magazine about law, edited by Harvard law students). Barack Obama graduated in 1991. He was elected to the Illinois State Senate in 1996, 1998, and 2002 and was elected to the US Senate in 2004 (Dem-IL). On November 4, 2008, Barack Obama won the general election, defeating John McCain (a Republican) to become the 44th President of the United States. His presidential inauguration was on January 20, 2009. President Obama won the Nobel Peace Prize in October 2009.

Barack Obama is a prime example of a bi-racial American child who could have had identity problems because of his heritage, his family structure and the commonalities of peer pressure that often occurs with these issues. Like most of his values, Barack learned empathy from his mother. She disdained any cruelty, thoughtlessness, or abuse of power, whether it expressed itself in the form of racial prejudice or bullying in the schoolyard. Whenever she saw a hint of such behavior in Barack, she would look him square in the eyes and ask, 'How do you think that would make you feel?' Years later, President Obama commented, as noted in *Obama Talks Back* by Gregory Reed "I find myself returning again and again to my mother's simple principle—'How would that make you feel,' as a guidepost for my politics."

Focusing on his studies rather than on his circumstances, Barack had navigated through the challenges of his youth and into the main arena as one of the most powerful men in the world.

As a bi-racial child, I encountered bullying, name-calling and taunting; but within the confines of my home, I always found comfort. Thanks to my parents, I gained confidence about whom I was and I learned to take pride in my heritage. Most importantly, I listened to my Dad, stayed in school and studied hard.

I didn't realize it until years later, but upon reflecting back, the preparation for my college education probably began as early as when I was in diapers. By the time I was in high school, I was at a good point to prepare for and succeed in college. One of the best ways to prepare for college is to understand what classes to take while you are in high school. And of course, keep going for A's and take challenging classes.

Regardless, the following classes are *musts* for you! The better your grades in these classes, the better your chances for college admission and financial aid assistance.

- ❖ 4 years of English
- ❖ 4 years of math (beginning with algebra)
- ❖ 2-3 years of history
- ❖ 3-4 years of a foreign language
- ❖ 2-3 years of science

When you begin your junior year at high school you should be clear about where you will be attending college—in state or out of state. However, you may not have a final decision about the particular college. The best thing to do is keep attending college fairs in your area. These events are the next best thing to actually visiting every school. Then you should narrow the application process to a minimum of three colleges and watch the deadlines!

As a high school student, I did not yet have a clear path about my journey or where I was going; but I am sure that God had already given me a purpose; I just needed to identify it. Little did I know, I was just a few years away from embarking upon that clear path.

After I had defined my mission through Make the Grade Foundation, I wanted to help students, who like myself, needed something or someone to impact their decision. I was able to offer that help via a guy named Ken Webb.

Since the late 1960s, native New Yorkers depended heavily on the voice of Ken 'Spider' Webb, one of New York's most popular morning radio personalities, to get them going early every morning with classic soul music, 'the color of the day', plenty of laughs and family humor. Ken raised WBLS-FM morning ratings to the #1 position, thus becoming a household name in the city. He then moved to RKO Broadcasting's WRKS-FM and brought its morning ratings to the #1 position for the very first time in that station's history, where it remained until 1995 when he returned to WBLS. While on the air, Ken exceeded exceptionally in the area of community service. He used his broadcast presence to raise needed funds for numerous community organizations, ranging from community causes to needy families. Ken has recently developed an Internet radio marketing and advertising company, Webb Internet Radio Network, which is made up of 12 Internet streaming channels and can be found at www.kenwebb.com.

In an effort to involve high school students in something that would gain their interest, Ken Webb and I went to one of the schools and asked, "Hey you guys like the Internet, right?" They all said, *Yah!* Then I said, "How would you like to do Internet radio? They said, *"How does it work?"* I told them, "You're gonna say something and I am gonna teach you how to program it so you can broadcast it." Those kids really got into it.

At Make the Grade Foundation we thrive on Success!

We have an Internet TV radio station with a group of about 10 students in a club. Every student has something different to say. We bring them all together, so they can make up the program.

Ken and I paid for all the equipment. The kids had bragging rights and started a brand new show. When we had a ribbon cutting ceremony, the kids prepared to broadcast. It was so amazing that I cried, mainly because I saw those kids change from "second chance" kids into winners. They had found something that they enjoyed, that they loved and they put together a show in front of us. It was amazing.

At Make the Grade Foundation, we reach the kids through different schools, different programs. There will always be some knuckleheads that we can't reach, but Make the Grade Foundation is making great strides with thousands of students every year.

I asked Mark S. Brantley, Esq., Chairman of the Board, Municipal Credit Union to offer some advice for students who had no direction or plan for their future. Mr. Brantley offered some key advice to help those students gain a foothold and get on the right path toward success. He stated: *Education is an investment in the "business of you." Any successful business must have a vision, a mission, a strategy/ strategic plan, and startup capital or an initial investment. Similarly, a student should view his/her own life as a "business" with a vision, mission and strategic plan.*

With the assistance of a parent, guardian or mentor, the initial investment can and should be in the student's education. Parents should start saving as early as possible toward their child's future. Upon entering middle school (i.e., grades 7-8), the student should begin to outline a plan for his/her higher education. It may sound complicated, but an educational business plan should simply consist of the following:

• The vision

What do you want to be? (doctor, lawyer, teacher, etc.)

• The mission

How do I make it happen? (relevant courses, vocational school or an academic college, full-time or part-time study)

• The strategy

What must I do to execute it? (Financial resource needs—scholarships vs. loans vs. work study, number of years of study, number of study hours/day, extracurricular activities).

Everything in the plan must be in alignment with the vision. For example, if you desire to be a pediatrician, then your mission (choice of school) should be in sync with that goal. Attending a trade school would run counter to that vision and would result in misalignment. Additionally, distractions that take the form of social overindulgences can also result in being out of sync. It can throw you off mission.

Once completed, the student should post the educational business plan in a conspicuous place. Be mindful that the plan is not etched in stone and the student may decide to change his/her vision. At the end of each semester, review the plan and assess your strengths, weaknesses, opportunities and threats (a SWOT analysis). In doing so, the student can seek additional help to strengthen weaknesses (e.g., tutoring), pursue opportunities (e.g., internships) and remove or avoid potential threats (e.g., bad influences).

Finally, look to credit unions as a potential funding source and educational investment partner. Credit union student loans are a great alternative to other traditional loans with rising interest rates. In the spirit of people helping people, credit unions have provided many scholarships.

Remember this, no matter what you do in life, always keep it real with yourself. Being honest about where you are and your circumstances will keep your mind focused and your feet sure. For example, if you know that your family is struggling financially with domestic issues, don't waste time wondering why or wallowing in self-pity, anger or pain. You can't change anyone but yourself, so acknowledge your position for exactly what it is, accept it no matter how much it hurts, and then take steps to improve your situation. The way to do that is through education.

SEVEN WAYS TO BECOME A BETTER STUDENT

1. My circumstances may have been the cause of some of the incidents that I encountered, but I would soon become more confident about whom I was and whom I could become.
2. Barack Obama was a good student, not necessarily a "model student", but he always aspired to be better.
3. Focusing on his studies rather than on his circumstances, Barack Obama navigated through the challenges of his youth and into the main arena as one of the most powerful men in the world.
4. As a high school student, I did not yet have a clear path about my journey or where I was going.
5. I wanted to help students, who like myself, needed something or someone to impact their decision.
6. Many of my encounters involved bullying incidents that stemmed from aggressive behavior from either older students or other young people my age.
7. Make sure you get involved in something that you really enjoy doing because you're going to have to work for a long time.

FOUR

The Community

What should young people do with their lives today? Many things, obviously. But the most daring thing is to create stable communities in which the terrible disease of loneliness can be cured.

—Kurt Vonnegut, Jr.

There was a time when your neighbors were in collaboration with your mom, or dad, or both parents to help raise a family. When you did something wrong, your neighbors didn't look the other way. Instead, they had permission to kick your butt a little bit and then they would tell your parents what you did. And when you got home, you were put on punishment. It's very important for people in our community to look out for our youngsters—to protect the community. All these things worked hand-in-hand while I was growing up and it was a great support system.

John Elmore, Esq., author of The African American Criminal Justice Guide stated, "It hurts me to see so many of our young men going to jail instead of college. Many go to jail, having been wrongfully convicted of crimes that they did not commit. Others will go to jail because of a lack of economic opportunities; and others go to jail simply because they did not have someone to show them."

Fortunately for me, Hank Carter created the basketball programs and boxing programs that I joined, and when he saw me doing something wrong he said, "Step out of line! Hey I saw that, you know better than that. I'll talk to your mother and father, they'll straighten you out." He always kept me in line like that, made sure I did the right thing, kept me on my *p*'s and *q*'s. It let me know that he cared about me.

We need more people like Hank, we need more of them to step up and be interested in our young people. If you look at the kids now, a lot of them are just going wild. With the unemployment rate, the kids can't get a job; so people assume they're worthless and that they can't keep themselves on track. And when a person doesn't care about themselves, they sure don't care about anyone else and that's a dangerous situation.

When I was about 12 or 13, I went through a period when I didn't care about myself. I had the hormonal stage and the adolescent things that you go through, all mixed together; but my support system came in there and held me down. It kept me together and helped me get grounded—my religious upbringing, my parents taking me out, and getting me involved in other things like sports. I saw the crime in my neighborhood, I saw people dying on benches from overdoses, shootings, stabbings, beatings, killings, and robberies. The horrors that I witnessed—and the ways my family and others got me through it—helped me out in later years. It gave me a unique perspective because I had experienced first-hand the good and bad that take place in a community.

As part of the Make the Grade Foundation's community outreach, I thought it was fitting for me to earn a Police Certificate. I went to officers' training school for 16 weeks. Gaining this insight has enabled me to understand exactly what the police officers in New York City and throughout the country go through to protect our communities. As in any other role, they are not all perfect, but for the most part our law enforcement officials make great sacrifices and lay their lives on the line every day, having to make split-second decisions.

Here is how my police training came about. I had been called to moderate as a host for programs that included people whose kids had gotten shot and killed. Many of the parents came together and set up a nonprofit organization. Once a year they highlight the memory of their son or daughter who may have been killed in their community, or the school will have a special memorial program.

One time after I had moderated at the Harlem State Office Building, Chief Phillip Banks, III and I were talking about the violence and gangs in the community. I was more than frustrated, and told him I was concerned that we keep having meetings like this, to no avail. I said I keep hosting them and they always turn out to be the same thing. We go home and we don't fix anything, and there's no follow-up and it's the same thing again. We do the program once a year in all five boroughs. People get shot and killed all over the place and we can't get to the root of the situation. Then I said, "I'll tell you what. I'm going to set up a meeting. Let's get together five or six community-based organizations and we'll come to your office at One City Plaza, downtown at Police Headquarters and we'll have a meeting and talk it over." So I did that and I brought a few of my board members from Make the Grade Foundation. We talked about a lot of pertinent issues.

When we left I told Chief Banks I wanted to get a better understanding of how the police department operates. He suggested attending the Citizens Police Academy, and I began classes the following Monday. I learned everything that the cadets who went to the academy did to become police officers.

Since I took the classes, I find myself verbally defending police officers, but I tell the kids, "Like any other job, there are police officers that are crooks too." Some are just out to get you. A police officer stopped me one day and said something inappropriate, but you've got to know what to do and what your rights are. He told me to do things that he really had no right to do without a warrant.

According to John Elmore, Esq., "There is another face of your friendly police officer. While the proportion of repeatedly abusive officers on any force is generally small, responsible authorities—including law enforcement supervisors, as well as local and federal government leader ship—often fail to act decisively to restrain or penalize such acts. Although, most police departments have strict guidelines on the use of deadly force, and international standards state that force should be used only as a last resort, proportionate to the threat and designed to minimize injury, it is clear that these standards are frequently breached and that too often the authorities have turned a blind eye to abuses."

So, before anything, it's important to abide by the law—to value your life and the lives of others. But on the other side of the coin, it's very important to understand the law, in case you get caught up in a situation that is not your fault. In that case, your reaction can mean life or death, or imprisonment (guilty or not).

Before I went to the Children's Village, I was always getting into trouble in the community. I was only about seven or eight years old, but a lot was going on in my young life. I'm not sure if it was related to learning the truth about Uncle Buddy's relationship to Cliff and me. That might have had something to do with it, but I believe it was more about what was happening *around* me—the environment I lived in. I almost died a number of times from innocent childhood pranks.

When I was about seven-years-old, someone had pulled a trunk out of a cellar. We were all playing with it. I climbed into the trunk and one of my friends closed the top; then he pulled the latch up and couldn't open it. The trunk had locked and I was inside, suffocating. So, my friend ran to my house and knocked on the door. Thank God, my dad just happened to be home for lunch. *It seemed like my dad was always there when I needed him.* He came downstairs with a hammer and a screwdriver and ripped that latch piece off and got me out of there. I could hardly breathe; so my dad gave me mouth-to-mouth resuscitation. Then, he got me out of the trunk and took me back home.

There were other things—bad places, bad times. But then you think about all the good times. Dad's brother had a house in Michigan, and nearby there was a dirt road that went way off into the woods. We weren't in the community but the community was still in us. Along the road, there was a campground and a little stream.

My brothers and I had our bow and arrows and hunting stuff with us. We were all shooting arrows into the air. I shot one arrow and I said "Oh, where did it go?" By that time, my brothers were catching frogs along the nearby creek. I said, "Watch out, the arrow's coming down! Here it comes! Here it comes! All of a sudden, we scattered. We started running in all directions; but the arrow was coming right down on top of me. At the last minute, I tripped and the arrow came right down on my leg and went about 5 or 6 inches into my foot. I left it in, because, I figured if I pulled it out, I would start bleeding too much. My brothers ran and got Dad who took me to the hospital. The doctor pulled out the arrow and sewed up the hole. It hurt so much and I thought about it for a long time. I even had nightmares because it could have killed any one of us.

I also had nightmares about the time when the police officer took my friend and me in the police van. That incident wasn't life or death, but it really impacted upon my life. The officer stepped on the gas and, in some odd way; I think he was purposely going fast. We were flying around the seat and very frightened…I guess you could say we were "scared straight".

The New York City Police Department has had a long history of helping youth through counseling and special workshops, but many of their deeds have gone unnoticed. For instance, Philip Banks Jr., a retired NYC Police Lieutenant, spent more than 27 years on the force before becoming the supervisor of criminal investigations in the Westchester County District Attorney's office. He is a former president of the New York City Chapter of the One Hundred Black Men, Inc., an organization that aims to improve the education and economic level of the African American community and its youth. He and his wife have raised three successful sons—a school principal, a Metropolitan Transportation Authority supervisor, and Chief Philip Banks III, who was the highest-ranking black officer in the NYPD.

At Make the Grade Foundation, I am working closely with the police department; we often meet with the Chief of Community Affairs and also work with Phillip Banks III. Chief Banks feels that whether you have sons or daughters, you should keep an open line of communication with them. They shouldn't be afraid to come to you, no matter what they think the outcome is going to be. If they don't talk to you, that means they're going to confide in someone else. Gangs have an attraction for these troubled kids. It then becomes a battle between the parents and the youth gangs. And if the gang's communication level surmounts yours, you're going to lose your kid. The attraction of a gang is that they make kids think they're family, and that the gang members are the only ones who care.

So your kids have got to know that you care about them, because once you lose them, it won't be easy to get them back. Make sure they know that having a big mouth can and will get them arrested. Many kids display a confrontational attitude, when confronted by police officers. When the officers ask them to leave a street corner, they are often greeted with tough looks and smart talk; then, the kids, in their machismo, walk away in a definitely slow manner. If they tick off a police officer off, he will find a reason to arrest them. Disturbing the peace, disorderly conduct, trespassing, blocking pedestrian traffic and loitering are discretionary charges that police officers can place on people because they have big mouths or are disrespectful. So, advise your kids not to pick a fight they can't win. If a neighborhood thug had a gun and a stick, you wouldn't be disrespectful to him because of your own common sense. Just because a guy has a uniform on, the rules do not change.

Make the Grade Foundation has allied with several community organizations like the One Hundred Black Men, Inc. To give our youth a totally inclusive package, we have interjected other priorities into our program. We also speak about the pitfalls associated with violence, shootings, bullying, sex, and drugs. We present them with hard options so they won't have an excuse to fail. And, when it comes to education and economics, we constantly bring in motivational programs to help students aspire to the next level.

The Department of Corrections has a program in place that is similar to ours at the Make the Grade Foundation. They also visit schools, so we asked if we could team up with them. However, in spite of all the programs being presented and the efforts to steer them straight, far too many of our youth are ending up in prison. I experienced first-hand the hardship of having a family member incarcerated, what it did to my mom and dad, and how it affected the entire family. It creates a lot of stress as well as a financial burden for attorney's fees and other related expenses. And, once these young people are caught up in the criminal justice system's web, you may never shake them loose.

Make the Grade Foundation, in association with WBLS Radio, visits local prisons in an attempt to get the message across to the inmates that all is not lost. A lot of kids are in prison—ages 16 and up. We try to inspire these younger inmates to look toward a brighter future.

For several years, I've been conducting talent shows in the prison system. There are 14 jails in New York City, on Rikers Island and the other five Boroughs. I go in and bring a sound system and the inmates come into the auditorium in two groups—one sits in one section –another sits in another section. We have an open mike with the inmates—adult inmates getting ready to go upstate. I ask for two comedians, an emcee, four singers, up to eight rappers (because they all like to rap) and I set it up like the Apollo Theater. Then we have a battle between the performers. I even get someone to act like Kiki Shephard, the longtime co-host of *It's Showtime at the Apollo*. A guy comes out walking like a woman, and everyone loves that. We also have a celebrity group come in to perform, maybe someone from the R & B Group, Blue Magic or a similar 1970s R & B act.

One time when we did our show, I had a secret weapon, the Persuaders. When it was time for them to come out to perform I learned that Flavor Flav was doing time in the same prison. Someone shouted," Flavor Flav is in the kitchen!" And I said, "Bring him out!" Flav came out in a chef's hat and apron and everybody went wild. So the Persuaders started singing "It's a Thin Line between Love and Hate" and Flav started singing with them. The guys went crazy. We had a good time that day—*I wish I had been able to record it*, but we couldn't bring in the video camera. He was doing time (cooking chicken) in the kitchen. Flav did a great job entertaining the fellas, but unfortunately, I couldn't document it.

William Jonathan Drayton, Jr. (born March 16, 1959), better known by his stage name Flavor Flav. Drayton (Flav) grew up in Freeport, Long Island, New York. His father owned a greasy spoon called the Soul Diner. *I guess that's where he acquired his gift of cooking; no wonder he landed in the prison kitchen.* Flav began playing the piano at age five. A musical prodigy, he sang in the youth choir at his church and mastered the piano, drums, and guitar at an early age. He eventually became proficient in 15 instruments. Flav attended Adelphi University in Long Island where he met Chuck D. They began rapping together and the rest is history. Flav rose to prominence in 1984 as a founding member of the rap group Public Enemy. By the time the political single "Fight the Power" was issued in 1989, the group had become mainstream superstars. Flav always appeared on stage and in public wearing big hats and glasses and a large clock dangling from his neck.

In 2002, Flavor Flav spent nine weeks in Rikers Island jail for driving with a suspended license, numerous parking tickets and showing up late for appointments with his probation officer. *That's when I met him.* After falling out of the public eye for a number of years, he reappeared in 2005 and beyond as the star of several VH1 reality series.

So Flavor Flav spent time in prison for child support, breaking probation and all that stuff. A message we try to give the inmates is, "*Let's take the time while we're doing time to get ourselves together.*" Judging from Flavor Flav's successes after he was released in 2002, I would say, he did just that. He got his act together, and although he has not stayed completely out of the clutches of the law, his lifestyle seems to have improved significantly.

When I go to the prisons, I like to have interaction, so I always ask the inmates, "How many of you have little youngsters at home?" Many of them raise their hands and I say, "Well guess what! You can't begin to take care of them until you take care of yourselves!" They get real quiet; some even get teary-eyed and the tears flow down their cheeks. You know they try to be hard in there, but when I talk about family and those little kids, it's difficult. I say, "Hey man, they need you; you can't do nothing in here. You gotta get out!"

Then I hear, "Well, when we get out, they won't give us no job." And I say, "Guess what! Start your own job. Go into business for yourself!" And then I tell them a story about a guy that I knew who used to pick up scrap metal. He had a shopping cart and picked up scrap metal from the highway, and he turned it in, and they'd give him money to bring in the metal. So then the guy got a van. He started throwing stuff in it, like mufflers, and put them in the back of his truck. Then he'd go to this place and they'd separate the metal; they'd take the aluminum and put it here and they'd take the iron and the steel and put it there. After a while, he started his own little business doing that. He got the land; he got the property and then he started expanding his business. Now, he has a huge company, he's very rich. You can start your own business doing that too, there's no excuse. You don't have to wait for someone to give you something. You can step out there and go get it. I said God gave you two feet, put one in front of the other and step to what you need to do. Just make sure it's legal!"

Having a degree is no guarantee that you will get a job; but creativity counts a lot. Once you get it, you have to keep striving and keep believing in yourself, especially today with the ever-increasing job shortage. Meeting Hal Jackson was such a blessing. It gave me my edge when I got out of college.

When Hal was asked what happened when Bob got involved with the station, Hal said, "I figured this young boy didn't really know what he wanted to do. So I took him by the hand and said come with me and learn what I'm doing, and then Bob started to develop an interest in communications. He saw what I did. It's pretty much like the Make the Grade Foundation's Shadow Program, except now Bob brings the kids in and mentors them."

Hal Jackson had a lot of broadcasting adventures to tell me about and through it all, I was like *wow!* Hal became my mentor and he was so smooth that I was not even aware that I was being mentored. He called me his protégé.

Hal was inside broadcasting more than I was, but he always believed in community and he supported everything that I did or wanted to do out in the community. Hal was no stranger to the needs of a helping hand. His life and story are fascinating; even after his death, Hal Jackson remains one of the most influential and most honored men in broadcasting. He not only broke color barriers on radio, he used his shows to promote charity work and created a Good Deeds Club. Off the air, Hal Jackson was always busy organizing and hosting charity events. His work earned him Presidential commendations from Roosevelt, Truman, and Kennedy.

Hal taught me that when I go into the community to *entertain, always leave them with something positive.*

Fortunately for so many of us, through various stages of our lives, we encounter great people like Hal Jackson. Three special women who have generously given their time, love and wisdom to the various communities they lived in are Vy Higginsen, Susan Taylor and Dorothy Pitman Hughes...because they cared, they shared.

Born and raised in Harlem, New York, Vy Higginsen is a highly recognized black pioneer among the city's media elite. She grew up in a community where show business was the norm and the entertainment industry was never out of her reach. Vy grew up focusing on the needs of her community.

Vy was the first black woman to produce a drama on Broadway with *Joe Tuner's Come and Gone* by August Wilson and she was the first black female writer, producer, director of the longest-running, Off-Broadway musical in the history of American theatre with *Mama, I Want to Sing*. The play opened March 23, 1983 in New York City and then had a two-and-a-half-year tour across the USA, seven tours throughout Japan and multiple appearances in the Caribbean, Germany, Switzerland, Austria and Italy. In 1998, Vy Higginsen created and **founded** the Mama Foundation for the Arts to present, preserve, and promote Gospel, Jazz, and the R&B arts for current and future generations. The Foundation identifies, trains, and employs the next wave of singers, musicians, administrators, and theater technicians. Recently, Vy was named a Harlem hero in Harlem as part of a public art and education project of Community Works, celebrating the living history of Harlem at the Schomburg Center for Research in Black Culture.

Susan Taylor was born in the Harlem neighborhood of New York City. After she founded Nequai Cosmetics for African American women, Susan heard that *Essence* magazine was looking for a beauty editor. Susan approached Editor-in-chief, Ed Lewis, for the position and was hired in 1970.and in 1981 she was promoted to editor-in-chief, a post she held until July 2000. Under Susan's guidance, *Essence* experienced phenomenal growth. Its monthly readership soared to more than 5 million, reaching black women all over the world. She became senior vice president in 1993. She was the host and executive producer of *Essence*, the country's first nationally syndicated African-oriented magazine television show, the Essence Awards show and the Essence Music Festival. After 37 years with Essence, Susan Taylor stepped down from her duties as editor-in-chief in order to devote more time to an organization she founded to help troubled children. She is an avid supporter of Edwin Gould Services for Children, a foster-care agency, and serves on the advisory board for Aid to Imprisoned Mothers. As an advocate for children and improving education, she once referred to failing schools as "the pipelines to prison." In 2006 Susan Taylor founded the National Cares Mentoring Movement with the goal of signing up more than one million people to become mentors.

Dorothy Pitman Hughes is a community activist, responsible for changing the lives of thousands of people throughout the world. Dorothy Pitman Hughes, the third child of six girls and two boys is a natural organizer, writer, speaker, activist and a lifelong champion for women, children and families. Dorothy spent her youth in Charles Junction, a small community in Lumpkin, Georgia immersed in the culture and legal constraints of Jim Crow. As a young adult, Dorothy moved to Harlem, New York where she worked as a domestic and sang in jazz clubs at night. In the 1970s Dorothy teamed up with Gloria Steinem, activist, feminist and founder of Ms. Magazine to do women's rights speaking tours. In 1979, Dorothy co-founded and organized New York City's Agency for Child Development, which currently provides care for over 250,000 children daily and employs thousands. She organized the first battered women's shelter in New York City, owned and operated three daycare centers and sponsored a successful youth entrepreneur apprentice project.

In 1998 Dorothy, then owner of Harlem Office Supply, initiated a stock offering that began with her vision and mission to involve inner-city people in the economic mainstream. Dorothy Pitman Hughes is the author of two books, which address the gentrification of Harlem: *Wake Up and Smell the Dollars! Whose Inner City Is This Anyway!* and *I'm Just Saying: It Looks like Ethnic Cleansing.* Dorothy Pitman Hughes currently resides in Jacksonville, Florida where she continues activist work to help empower underserved citizens.

To these women, life would have been meaningless if they had not recognized their calling and embarked on their designated journeys through life. While always thinking of others, they created their legacies and their service to the community made an impact on everyone they encountered. Their outreach is immeasurable as their good deeds spread far beyond the communities of their birth.

Sometimes when you feel like you're not doing enough, you reach out to the community to give back. That's one of the reasons I wanted to go on the radio, to express myself to the community. And then in college, I still wanted to go on the radio. But when I got the radio gig and started broadcasting, I realized, *My God, I'm here by myself. I'm talking on the microphone to the masses, but I need to get out there and talk to people in the community. I need to look into their eyes.* That's the same thing that happened when I quit my printing job. I was up at night, I ran that machine faster than anyone else because I knew how to mix chemicals and dye before it got to the other side of the press. I was good at my job but that wasn't enough. It wasn't fulfilling me spiritually. I thought, *I'm here by myself, but I need to be out there where the people are. That's where it's at, helping people get what they need out of life.* That's my purpose. That's what I love to do. Make the Grade Foundation has filled a void in my life by bringing the community to my door, one of the seven components toward the success of the program.

SEVEN WAYS TO MAKE
A DIFFERENCE IN YOUR COMMUNITY

1. I think it's very very important for the people in our community to look out for our youngsters.
2. Nearby there was a dirt road that went way off into the woods; we weren't in the community but the community was still in us.
3. In a community that cared for all who lived there, that community can nurture your childhood.
4. Sometimes you may feel like you're not doing anything, so you reach out to the community to give back.
5. Your service to the community can make an impact on everyone you encounter.
6. Listen to elders in your community and develop strategies to help families thrive.
7. *I need to get out there and talk to people in the community—I need to look into their eyes.*

FIVE

The Clergy

Blessed are those who can give without remembering and take without forgetting.

—Anonymous

One of the most important components of Make the Grade Foundation is the Clergy. Very few things will work without God in your life.

Because of separation of church and state, Make the Grade Foundation doesn't talk about the church inside the schools; but when we have our career fairs and college fairs, sometimes the programs are held in different churches and we have a chance to talk about religion.

I also mention God every night, when I get off the air or when I wrap up a show. I believe that when you are born you already have all your blessings, but a lot of people just say, "I'm waiting on God." Well, God already gave your blessings to you, but you just have to activate them. So once you activate your blessings, anything is possible; you can go as far as you want to go, you're unstoppable. *God gave you two feet. Put one in front of the other and step to what you need to do.*

I remember when I was a little kid, my father was a doorman in Forest Hills Rego Park. He got off at midnight. While leaving his job, we always came out the back way and through the dark alley. It was so dark that it gave me the chills walking through there...I was so afraid. My father always took me by the hand and he said, "I have your hand, just walk with me," and he put my little hand into his big hand and held it while we walked through that dark alley and up the ramp. I felt very secure and comfortable because I knew that my father had me by the hand; and that's when I realized God was there before us.

We know that many of our youth have problems so we go in and speak to the students to motivate them. The ministers participate because we need to complete that circle; we need all those entities involved. We need the parents, we need the teachers, we need the community, and we need the ministers.

The biggest motivators of people are the department of education, the churches and the media—TV and radio. Many young people start singing the songs they hear on the radio…that may or may not be good for them. But the churches have the greatest power to motivate these young people, especially when the congregations join together in song.

The Clergy that we have invited to participate in Make the Grade Foundation are open-minded and deeply entrenched in the issues confronting the youth. For instance, a lot of people wouldn't come out and talk about AIDS but certain clergy would; that's whom I want involved with our program. The most important issue is that in order to be successful you have to speak out and help others get what they need out of life …and in helping others, your success comes. I think one of the paradoxes of life is that *you get when you give.*

My message is relevant right now because a lot of things are happening right now—this will be the end of the world as we know it. It will not be the end of the world where people are dead and gone, but things are changing so rapidly right now that we've got to know it and go back to basics. Where we need to go now, more than ever before, is back to the church.

Whether they have participated in one of my programs at events, expos or in schools, I give the kids a very important message to leave with. It's the same message I use to wrap up my TV or radio show. I always say: *Remember this, what you are, is God's gift to you and what you make of yourself is your gift to God. So choose your choice, and let your choice control the choosing."* I throw my quote in at the end of every appearance, in spite of the fact that the school system doesn't want me to be preaching because of *Separation of Church and State.* The Separation is formally described as the distance in the relationship between organized religion and the nation state.

The right to freedom of religion is so central to American democracy that it was enshrined in the First Amendment to the Constitution along with other fundamental rights, such as freedom of speech and freedom of the press. The First Amendment stated that "Congress shall make no law respecting an establishment of religion, or prohibiting the free exercise thereof..." Therefore, in order to guarantee an atmosphere of absolute religious liberty, this country's founders also mandated the strict separation of church and state. Largely because of this prohibition against government regulation or endorsement of religion, diverse faiths have flourished and thrived in America since the founding of the republic. James Madison, the father of the United States Constitution, once observed that "the [religious] devotion of the people has been manifestly increased by the total separation of the church from the state."

No clergy are involved in programs at the public schools because of restrictions, but Make the Grade Foundation frequently goes to church schools. Throughout the years, I have conducted programs at Catholic schools and Christian schools. I don't necessarily want to bring religion into public schools, but I want to make church a component relating to what I feel is needed to make a child successful.

That's a very sticky situation for some people, but that's what we want to let our youth know. The Church component can be controversial. In response to our fundraising efforts, we've been told, "Well you know that a lot of people don't give money to that type of situation." To me, it's very disappointing that sometimes, when you're affiliated with the church, people don't want to be supportive.

I believe wholeheartedly that young people need to know there's someone responsible for them being here on earth other than their mother and father. They need to have faith and find out there is a God. As a child, I was baptized Catholic, received my confirmation, was brought up in the Catholic church and served as an altar boy for several years. My faith in God is deeply rooted.

When my dad died in 1995, I missed him terribly and often reflected back to the days that he would help me overcome my fear by taking my hand as we walked in the darkness.

In 1997 I think I had an epiphany; it was about two years after my dad died. I went to Las Vegas on a business trip. Since I had a little free time, I called my son and invited him to come to Vegas to hang out with me—he lived in Oakland at the time—but, because of his job, he couldn't come. So I said, *"I'll come to you."* I rented a car and began my journey. I went to the Grand Canyon and I drove by the Hoover Dam. While I was driving through the Mojave Desert heading up to Los Angeles, the sun stopped shining. It got very dark and looked like little tornadoes blowing around in the near distance. It was eerie, I had never had that feeling before and I thought, *where's my father's hand?* It was so dark. I said, *oh my God, I can't see 100 feet in front of me.*

I pulled into a rest stop. There was a store, so I went to get some gum and snacks, and the lady behind the counter said, "Are you traveling by yourself? Be careful in these parts." I wondered, *how did she know I was traveling alone?* The desert was so lonely, and I had a very eerie feeling. After a while things started clearing up. Finally at the end of my 18 hour journey, I made it to Oakland. I pulled into a 7-11 store and gave my son a call (I didn't have a cell phone back then). My son didn't answer the phone, so I went to his apartment and put a note on his door, which said, "Shi give me a call at the phone booth, I'm downstairs by the 7-11".

I waited by the phone booth until around 1:00 A.M. and suddenly I looked up at a billboard hanging across from the store and saw my dad....up on the billboard! There was a message written alongside his image, "We're Cingular, wireless and I'm with you every step of the way." I immediately called my sister and told her that Dad was on the billboard and she asked me *how did they get his picture?* I said, "I don't know!" I went into the store and got two cameras and took a bunch of pictures. Then I waited a little longer for my son but he still didn't show up. I was real upset and decided to head back to Vegas; but I left there in a serene state of mind and I was okay. I said to myself, *I came here to see my son, but instead, I saw my father and the Holy Spirit.* And I kept thinking about it all the way back to Vegas.

I was still upset with my son, so I didn't call him until I got back home to New York. I knew I had the camera, so I developed my film from Oakland and then went to my sister's house where I saw my sister and brother. But when I developed the film, nothing came out;

so I called my son and asked him, *"Isn't there a 7-11 down the street from you?"* He told me 'yes'. I told him *"Go look and tell me what you see!"*—He looked and said, "Grandpa!" I said to my sister, *"See, I'm not crazy!"* Then my son read the billboard, "We're Cingular, wireless and I'm with you every step of the way." He took some pictures and they also came out blank.

I spoke about the incident at a church two years later and the minister called it an 'epiphany'. He said, "God lets you know He's there with you whatever you want to do." He called it ashoke. "There may be roads you've got to go down, maybe hard bumpy roads. You may go through deserts; the visibility's gonna be low. You may drop to your knees, but He's with you every step of the way."

One of the many clergy that I know personally and whom I have known throughout my radio career is Alfred Charles "Al" Sharpton, Jr. aka Reverend Al Sharpton. I recently saw Reverend Al at Hal Jackson's "Celebration of Life" service, he delivered the eulogy.

Reverend Al Sharpton is not known for his specific church affiliation, but rather for his views and advocacy. He is an American Baptist minister, civil rights activist, and television/radio talk show host who speaks out and acts, without hesitation, on issues that affect the rights of African Americans. According to Reverend Sharpton, "An activist's job is to make public civil rights issues until there can be a climate for change."

Reverend Al Sharpton established the National Youth Movement in 1971 when he was 16 years old. After Jesse Jackson left the Southern Christian Leadership Conference over his administrative suspension, Sharpton—who was mentored by Jackson—also left the SCLC in protest and formed the National Youth Movement. The mission of the organization was fighting drugs and raising money for impoverished children in the inner cities.

Al formed the organization, and shortly thereafter met James Brown's son Teddy, who tragically got killed in a car accident in upstate New York. Teddy and Al were the same age, sixteen. When James Brown came to New York he heard about this young preacher that Teddy had befriended, so he decided to do a memorial concert in memory of his son for Al's youth organization. James Brown became like the father Al didn't have after his parents separated.

In 1971 Al became a tour manager for James Brown, who financed his National Youth Movement. What Al does functionally is what Doctor King, Reverend Jackson and the movement are all about; but James Brown taught him about manhood and how to take adversity and use it to his advantage.

Al Sharpton Jr. was born October 3, 1954 in Brooklyn, New York, to Alfred Charles Sharpton, Sr. and Ada Sharpton. The church that Al grew up in, Washington Temple Church of God in Christ in Brooklyn, was a hot spot for gospel singers. It was probably a mega-church before there actually were mega-churches. In the late fifties and early sixties Bishop F.D. Washington, who was the bishop of the church, had about 5,000 members. All the gospel greats would come to the church. Al Sharpton started preaching at four and because he was the "Wonderboy Preacher", and had his own little church celebrity, he got to know all the gospel singers. In 1964 when the World's Fair came to New York, Mahalia Jackson had Al preach and she sang there that night. Then Al toured a few other cities with her. When Al was around nine years old his father left home. The family had to move from their middle class community to the public housing projects in the Brownsville neighborhood of Brooklyn. Al Sharpton graduated from Samuel J. Tilden High School in Brooklyn, and attended Brooklyn College, dropping out in 1975, after just two years.

Reverend Al Sharpton is known throughout the world for his chant "No Justice! No Peace!" as he led numerous marches on behalf of civil rights and a broken justice system. His life has been threatened many times and in 1991 he was stabbed in the chest during a march in Bensonhurst, New York. After Sharpton recovered from his wounds, he asked the judge for leniency for the offender when he was sentenced.

Sharpton's supporters consider him "a man who is willing to tell it like it is". Former New York Mayor Ed Koch, a one-time foe, once said that Sharpton deserves the respect he enjoys among African Americans: "He is willing to go to jail for them, and he is there when they need him."

In early 1991 the Reverend Sharpton founded the National Action Network in Harlem, New York. NAN fights to empower people by providing extensive voter education, services aiding the poor, supporting economically small community businesses, and confronting racism and violation of civil and human rights.

In 2004, Reverend Al Sharpton was a candidate for the Democratic nomination for the U.S. presidential election. In November 2005, Sharpton signed with Radio One to host a daily national talk radio program, which began airing on January 30, 2006 entitled *Keepin It Real with Al Sharpton* and he makes regular guest appearances on Fox News (such as *The O'Reilly Factor*), CNN, and MSNBC. Rev. Al has recently been named the host of MSNBC's *PoliticsNation*, a nightly talk show, which premiered on August 29, 2011.

Reverend Al Sharpton is but one example of the African American clergy, living and journeying throughout the United States for centuries, who have no fear of expanding their mission from the pulpit into our communities. The youth who encounter these brave "preachers" gain more than spiritual healing; they gain a wealth of knowledge about how to stand by their principles and how to seek truth as it applies to justice and freedom.

SEVEN THOUGHTS ABOUT YOUR RELATIONSHIP WITH THE CLERGY AND GOD

1. One of the most important components of Make the Grade Foundation is the Clergy.
2. Once you activate your blessings, anything is possible; you can go as far as you want to go, you're unstoppable.
3. *God gave you two feet. Put one in front of the other and step to what you need to do.*
4. *Remember this, what you are is God's gift to you and what you make of yourself is your gift to God.*
5. I don't necessarily want to bring religion into public schools, but I want to make church a component relating to what I feel is needed to make a child successful.
6. I believe wholeheartedly that young people need to know there's someone responsible for their being here on earth other than their mother and father.
7. Young people need to have faith and find out there is a God.

SIX

The Health Component

As I see it, every day you do one of two things:
build health or produce disease in yourself.
                                                                —Adelle Davis

Healthy eating means healthy living—that's why Make the Grade Foundation has the health component. A friend of mine died recently—she was 103-years-old and in great health. In spite of her age, she never really had any health problems. Nothing ever really bothered her—high cholesterol, heart problems, diabetes—nothing. When she moved into a senior care home, she was surprised when she saw the condition of the other people there. She said, "Wow, am I supposed to be in a wheelchair?"

My dad was like that too; he lived to the age of 95. He ate well and walked almost every day. My friend Hal Jackson lived to be 97-years-old. He was also the picture of health until the day he died. Hal exercised and had good eating habits, as well. He read every day to keep his mind active and said, "I've got to keep working." Hal Jackson could still be heard every Sunday on WBLS-Radio until three weeks before he passed away. When Hal was 96-years-old, I traveled to Mexico with him and he didn't miss a beat.

The Make the Grade Foundation Health Component is something that came to me as an important piece of the puzzle. For a number of years, I have wanted to understand how to keep the body as pure as possible. That's the reason I am now back in school studying for my PhD at The American Institute of Holistic Theology. I am majoring in the philosophy of metaphysics dealing with natural healings.

With all the things that are happening around us, including: pollutions in the air, pollutions in our clothes and the changes in our food, our bodies are forced to work harder to get the nutrients we need to stay alive. I get into a lot of debates in an effort to raise awareness about diabetes. The body cannot correct itself if it doesn't have the nourishment it needs and if the proper foods are not there. Unfortunately, the pollution is always there in the air that we breathe, especially in New York.

Healthy eating, healing with foods, and doing the proper things are essential because the body heals itself when you treat it right. Sometimes when you are too far out there, it takes a longer time to heal because you continue doing the same things over and over. So, as your body heals you've got to change your lifestyle, your eating habits and your sleeping habits and this will change your body by giving it the nutrients that it needs. Unfortunately, if you do go too far you have to visit a doctor, but the doctor never bothers to find out the root of the problem, or what happened when this problem started. Doctors seldom ask themselves questions, such as: *What's the root of this? What's happening? Why is this happening?*

Healthy Minds

Without a whole lot of pressure from you or your family, the doctor is not going to try to find out what the problem is. He's only going to put a Band-Aid on it and depending on the problem, will give you a topical solution—chemotherapy, a chemical solution or pills—to try to get rid of the problem. The truth is, you may get rid of the problem for a little while, but if you don't get to the root, it's very likely going to re-occur. I am interested in trying to find out how to keep the body, mind and spirit healthy.

In ancient times—biblical times—people got into dreams. God came to people in their dreams. The ancient people and the Native Americans really believed in these dreams; but today, we don't pay much attention to the stuff that comes to us through our dreams and that happens in our subconscious world. Ideas come into our dreams and try to correct our personality and our character in our conscious world. But, if we don't make those corrections, we go to the doctor trying to make those changes because we don't pay any attention to our subconscious.

Healthy Eating

When it comes to the Make the Grade Foundation's health component, we teach you how to take care of your body by eating right and exercising every day, as much as you can. There are so many foods out there that are no good for us. Everything is pasteurized, everything is homogenized, processed and whatever other names they give to it. Definitely read the labels, you'll know exactly what I am talking about. They also take all the nutrients out of food, so eat healthy, exercise, live healthy and try to do the right things for your body.

Childhood Obesity

The biggest health issue that Make the Grade Foundation deals with is childhood obesity. I have two Make the Grade vans and a team of people that I work with. We go around and participate in health fairs throughout the Tri-State area (New York, New Jersey and Connecticut).

We always discuss childhood obesity and how important it is to eat healthy. Obesity now affects 17% of all children and adolescents in the United States—triple the rate from just one generation ago. Achieving and maintaining a healthy weight isn't just about a "diet" or "program." It is part of an ongoing lifestyle that you can adopt now and stay with for years to come.

A good way to keep your weight under control is to participate in physical activities. Health experts recommend that all teens should be active every day as part of play, sports, work, transportation, gym class, or planned exercise. Three or more times each week, teens should do something that requires moderate to high levels of exertion for 20 minutes or more. This may include jogging, brisk walking, swimming, skating, aerobic dance, tennis, and full-court basketball. There will be a major difference in how you look and feel.

A teen's concern about his or her athletic ability may sometimes lead to problems. For example, teens who are involved in activities that require weight management (such as ballet, wrestling, and gymnastics) may be at a greater risk for the eating disorders anorexia nervosa (self-starvation) or bulimia (binge and purge). Some teens use steroids to build muscle or improve their athletic ability. These are potentially life-threatening behaviors and should be avoided.

Body Piercing and Tattoos

Something else that has gained popularity, but should be avoided because of possible injury, is body piercing. This is a risk-taking behavior that is gaining wide acceptance because of an increasing number of adolescents engaging in the companion art form of tattooing at a younger age. School nurses are beginning to see more students with health problems associated with the piercing of various body parts.

Puberty

In the auditorium, people are embarrassed to discuss drugs, sex and health, but we talk about it anyway. Discussing sex and the repercussions that come with it, such as pregnancy and sexually transmitted diseases is particularly difficult for the kids who are entering puberty. Preteens and teens are often embarrassed by their changing bodies and concerned that they are not developing at the same rate as their friends. For girls, puberty begins around 10 or 11 years of age and ends about age 16. Boys enter puberty later than girls-usually about 12 years of age-and it lasts until about age 16 or 17. Girls and boys usually begin puberty about the same time their mothers and fathers did. We encourage parents to talk with their children about the physical changes that will happen during puberty and to reassure their children that young people grow and develop at their own pace and that the changes are normal.

Vaccinations

The best way to protect your adolescent against diseases such as measles, mumps, rubella (MMR), diphtheria, tetanus (also known as lockjaw), hepatitis B (a serious infection that can lead to diseases of the liver) and varicella (chicken pox) is vaccination. Because of vaccinations, there are fewer cases of these diseases, but they still exist.

ADHD

One of the most common conditions that affect children today is attention deficit hyperactivity disorder. At times, children with this condition exhibit uncontrolled behavior. Between four and eight percent of children have ADHD, although it is three times more common in boys. Kids with ADHD often have trouble focusing or concentrating, and they might shout out answers without raising their hand, lose things, interrupt people, or fidget and move around a lot.

If a major stress or event has occurred in a child's life, he or she may exhibit ADHD symptoms for a period of time, although they have not developed ADHD. A death in the family, illness, divorce or change in environment can negatively affect a child's behavior and health. When my brother Cliff and I were transferred from the public school system to Children's Village, it was erroneously suggested that we might have ADD (the term used at that time for Attention Deficit Disorder). Our failure to focus in class had nothing to do with genetics, but rather with the stress from the desegregation of schools and our "Uncle Buddy's" shocking story. We were fortunate enough that our parents would not allow anyone to medicate us unnecessarily.

Treatment is generally considered if symptoms affect daily living or schoolwork. People with ADHD may take certain medicines or get therapy or counseling. Dealing with ADHD is a difficult task, but with proper attention to symptoms and treatment, and consistent follow-up, parents can help their children who have this disorder to succeed. Children with ADHD do not act out intentionally. They are not in control of their behavior. Our ADD was dealt with in a similar fashion, but instead of acting out, we tended to be more depressed and introverted.

There is no cure for ADHD, but it can be controlled. Most researchers believe ADHD is partially genetic, as it is common within families. It might also be related to drugs, smoking or alcohol use when the mother is pregnant, although this has not been confirmed. A premature birth, low-birth weight or brain injury during birth may also lead to ADHD development. Usually, kids are diagnosed with the problem between ages six and twelve, when the condition starts to affect schoolwork and studying.

When we talk in the auditorium, as part of the discussion, we always encourage kids to exercise their mind, body and spirit to prepare themselves for everyday life. We tell them to pick up something and read it. You don't have to be in school to pick up a book, newspaper or magazine and read; you can always pick up something during break. Stay informed. Talk to knowledgeable people in general. You don't have to be in school, but, to exercise your mind; you can talk to people in authority, people with something intelligent to say. You need to educate yourself every day, in every way possible.

There are two nurses in my family. One of my daughters is a nurse; she recently got her degree after retiring from the U.S. Navy and I have a niece who is an R.N. I have another niece in the medical field as a medical assistant and my older sister Lianna takes care of my mom. Lianna is a clinical social worker; she knows about the body, as well.

One of my other sisters, Ida, passed away from cancer and my youngest brother died from HIV-AIDS during the 80s epidemic. Considering how much I know about good health habits and how important taking care of the body is, both situations were extremely stressful to me.

About the time my brother died, the drugs they had for HIV-AIDS were very toxic—they didn't have all the cocktails they have today. The disease was killing people from all walks of life, particularly those involved in the entertainment industry. A lot of people didn't have the opportunity to be scared; HIV-AIDS is a silent killer that just sneaked up on them with no warning. My brother was a party animal; he had unprotected sex, as too many of our kids do today. They see STDs now as just a shot of penicillin and they continue to act the way they always did, without taking precautions. We try to spread the word that they MUST take precautions and we try to teach them the whys and the hows.

I was an athlete and always health conscious, but I became even more health conscious because of the deaths of my siblings. I was also into biology and chemistry, always interested in how the body works and how to keep the mind, body and spirit healthy.

Because of the importance of eating a good breakfast, Make the Grade Foundation started the Breakfast Program several years ago—I have the original commercials. We are now doing a Breakfast Program with Steve Harvey, which he got involved with about two years ago.

I am also the Producer and Host of "Daily Dose", a one-minute segment that runs on both radio stations five times a day as well as on WBLS.com and WLIB.com. The radio station selected me to do it because they know I'm working on a PhD for healthy living. I can't officially prescribe anything to you, but I can make suggestions such as: *Hey you might want to try this.* We started the "Daily Dose" in Harlem Hospital with WBLS. I began the program there because, when we were working with Harlem Hospital and the Uptown Chamber of Commerce, I came up with something called Healthy Eating and Healthy Living Initiative.

Our Make the Grade vans are used to educate and inform the kids about emergency lifesaving techniques and they are equipped with sound systems and video screens. Whenever we do health fairs, The Bedford Stuyvesant Volunteer Ambulance Corp works with Make the Grade Foundation to also teach CPR to the families in the community, not just to the kids. We teach CPR right on site so people can see how to do it. Make the Grade Foundation also offers special classes at various sites where the kids learn CPR. Those classes are done on location in juvenile centers, plus we take small groups to visit hospital emergency rooms. The volunteers take the kids through all the steps necessary for saving lives.

I often think back to my trunk episode and how my Dad saved my life because he knew CPR. It makes me realize how important it is to provide that knowledge to the young people today.

I remain excited about the many programs that Make the Grade Foundation offers as part of our health component because it not only shapes young lives; in many instances it saves them. We talk about health and well-being in the schools and bring the vehicles around to keep the programs interesting. The programs are very well-received. They have affected and changed thousands of lives in our communities.

Here are some quick facts that could affect your teen's well-being. Discussing these facts and their associated perils could save your teen's life:

○ Injuries kill more teens than all diseases combined.

○ Car crashes are one of the leading causes of death and disability among teens today.

○ At least one teen dies of an injury every hour every day in the United States.

○ Other causes of injury or death among teens include drowning, sports injuries, and rape.

○ More teens are being killed by guns than ever before.

○ Most teens do not like and do not wear bike helmets.

○ Adolescents are less likely to use seat belts than any other age group.

○ Understanding and obeying the rules of the road are important components of safe cycling.

○ Alcohol is involved in about 35% of teen driver fatalities.

As parents, it is important to know how to get the best health care services for your children. A great resource in New York City is the Joseph P. Addabbo Family Health Center, which is among the top 5% of nationally ranked providers. Addabbo's mission is to be the leading preventive and comprehensive primary health care center in New York. The people at Addabbo work individually and collectively, through education, innovation, and community partnership to anticipate and exceed the expectations of their patients, the community, and each other. Under the direction of Doctor Peter Nelson, CEO, the Joseph P. Addabbo Family Health Center continues to attract and retain the highest quality staff as they promote personal health, growth, and empowerment. Doctor Nelson has enlightened us on some of the most important aspects of The Obama Care Bill, which is currently signed into law.

Obama Care aims to improve community health care centers in an effort to improve health care for those who cannot afford private health care. It does not replace private insurance or Medicaid, which will be reformed and expanded in order to help cover more people, especially those below the poverty level.

ObamaCare, Obama Care and Health Care for America are all the same thing; an extension of the "Patient Protection and the Affordable Care Act" and ongoing efforts to reform the health care industry. Some aspects of Obamacare health care reform are already enacted. The Patient Protection and Affordable Care Act, signed 2 years ago, requires that insurance plans cover preventative services and stops insurance companies from dropping you when you are sick as well as offering a number of other reforms and protections.

The ObamaCare bill that handles workplace reform helps to ensure equal care for all Americans. One of the main goals of ObamaCare is to ensure that all preventative care will be free on all insurance plans. ObamaCare costs what people can afford. The Obama Care Health Care Reform Plan or Health Care for America Plan will cost the average American around $70. For those Americans who cannot afford this premium and whose income is at or over 200% below the national poverty level, there will be a free option and subsidies. This ensures that Health Care for America covers every American and can be sustained by the people of the United States of America and Our Government. For most Americans, this means better coverage for less money, for many it means having coverage over no or poor coverage; for others it means paying a little more to ensure healthcare for America's poorest.

Affordable health coverage means Americans and their families pay what they can afford. Thirty-two million Americans who currently do not have health insurance will be covered under the Health Care for America Plan. Insurance companies will no longer deny children coverage based on preexisting conditions and by 2014, insurance companies would not be able to deny anyone with preexisting conditions. Also, parents will have to allow children to stay on their parents' health insurance plans until they are 26.

With all the health components of our programs, along with the long-term benefits of ObamaCare, we feel that more young people and their families will be able to Make the Grade by gaining and maintaining a healthier lifestyle.

SEVEN WAYS TO GAIN
A HEALTHY PERSPECTIVE ON LIFE

1. Healthy eating means healthy living.
2. School nurses are beginning to see more students with health problems associated with the piercing of various body parts.
3. Health experts recommend that all teens should be active every day as part of play, sports, work, transportation, gym class, or planned exercise.
4. Healthy eating, healing with foods, and doing the proper things are essential because the body heals itself when you treat it right.
5. *Obama Care aims to improve community health care centers in an effort to improve health care for those who cannot afford private health care.*
6. It is important to know how to get the best health care services for your children.
7. A death in the family, illness, divorce or change in environment can negatively affect a child's behavior.

SEVEN
Financial Literacy

Financial literacy is an issue that should command our attention because many Americans are not adequately organizing finances for their education, healthcare, and retirement.

—Ron Lewis

When I was very young, my dad taught me how to value and respect money. He would come home from his railroad job, pull out all his tips, dump a bunch of change on the table, and we'd count it together. First and foremost, before he allocated any change to us kids, he would suggest what we should do with the money, with emphasis on saving some. He always allowed us to borrow money from him and gave us terms to repay our loan. This set a standard for the time when I was ready to attend college and apply for my student loan. I understood my financial responsibility and thanked my dad for those early lessons he taught me.

Years later, I also had a great mentor in Percy Sutton. When it came to the concept of financial literacy, he taught me about the importance of always having a backup plan and the benefit of owning several businesses, in case one failed. To this day, I rely on his wisdom to guide me through many of my financial decisions.

It's important to know basic math and how it applies to everyday living and your future success, so Make the Grade Foundation places a high value on financial literacy. Some of the schools we visit have a special program to teach younger students about saving money, but in the higher grades—when students need it the most—they aren't being taught the finer points that are necessary to financially sustain them throughout their lives.

For most adolescents, their first financial hurdle is college. College tuition is a huge expense for any family; it's like paying for a mortgage. When many of our students graduate from college they are already in debt. Their parents may not have been able to save for their college education, or perhaps they didn't save enough.

Some children are fortunate to have mentors or family members who are very conscientious about financial literacy and they begin to educate their children early. From the time they are toddlers, children can learn by playing number games and paying the cashier when purchases are being made at the store. Family members can teach them more about financial success as it becomes appropriate for their age level.

Important financial concepts to learn include:

- O Opening a checking account and a savings account
- O Saving money, balancing a budget, and paying bills on time
- O Establishing a relationship with bank employees
- O Applying for scholarships, financial aid, educational loans, credit cards, and mortgages
- O Understanding the value of home ownership versus renting
- O Finding income streams available to young people
- O Developing a high credit score
- O Building a respectable reputation in the world of credit

I asked financial entrepreneur and CNN commentator Ryan Mack for advice about the subject of financial literacy for children. He is the founder of All About Business, a global program under the umbrella of the Optimum Institute of Economic Empowerment. This nonprofit organization is geared towards the spread of empowerment through social movement and grassroots advocacy. Their purpose is to cultivate talent and encourage youth to become active members of the community through leadership, philanthropy, and professional responsibility. Ryan had some great advice:

Financial Literacy

Talk to your children about the principles of financial literacy as early as age 6 or 7. By the time they are in 1st or 2nd grade they should begin to have conversations about the allocation of money. When I was little, I used to think there was someone inside the ATM machine dispensing money. My mother said, "No, I have to work to put money into my bank account in order to get money out of the bank." Having conversations like that can let children see the importance of banking.

Allowance

Another good conversation is about allowance. You can set up three boxes labelled "spend it," "save it," and "give it away." Every time you give your children money for allowance have a conversation about the amount they will "deposit" into each box. When your children want to buy something with their money, ask questions such as: "Is it really important? Do you really need that? Is it better to wait and save for something else more important?" Getting your children to think about where their money is going can lead to a larger conversation about budgeting before spending.

Savings Account

To open a savings account, find out the minimum amount required by your bank. A 529 credit reserve account is tax deductible and can be a great option for saving money. Take the "save it" box to the bank to open an account, and when your children see extra money showing up on their monthly statements you can discuss the concept of interest. Let them know that the bank will pay them for putting their money into a savings account.

Inflation

In simple terms, you can discuss inflation by having a conversation about why a candy bar cost 5 cents back in Grandfather's day and why it now costs a dollar. Let them know that, essentially, the dollar that you have in your pocket, as long as you hold it in your pocket, is losing value; it used to buy 20 candy bars, and now it only buys one. Your children's purchasing power is becoming less, so in order to profit they should put some of their money in the bank to earn interest.

The Power of Money

You can also talk to your children about the power of money. Instead of buying an expensive toy or computer game for your children, purchase it with the understanding that they will "owe" you for it. But instead of paying you back the money, you can have them earn it. Give them chores around the house and place a dollar value on each chore. They can earn their way out of the debt; for instance, $3 for vacuuming, $1 for cleaning their room or for taking out trash, $5 to do the dishes. Put the list on the refrigerator and keep track so the children can see when it will be paid off. After the debt is paid in full, tear up the "IOU" and celebrate their achievement.

Stock Investments

Ryan Mack also recommends that students learn about stock at an early age, even though investing may seem far off in the future. However, his advice to students is "wait until you have a steady stream of sustainable and consistent income; then every single month you can invest in a portfolio for dollar cost average." You don't know what level of income you will have so I tell young people not to buy idle stock (funds are simply funds that are not deposited in an interest bearing or investment tracking vehicle). It's better to be an active investor rather than an active trader. In other words, you should be in a position to put money into your account every month on a consistent basis to effectively employ dollar cost budgeting. If you can't invest every month, don't invest at all—wait until you can afford to be consistent. A lot of students can't be active investors because they have accumulated so much debt by the time they graduate.

Career Portfolio

A career portfolio should consist of a resume, cover letter, marketing plan, community outreach program, newsletter, pictures, and awards, along with a high school or college diploma. For instance, if your child is interested in going to law school, he or she could write about law, hold workshops in the community, or do a blog on Facebook. Children can print their blogs and make a "career portfolio," which they can use later to earn scholarships. I know a child who was writing about dinosaurs on YouTube and gained national attention. Children as young as age 10 should start writing in a journal about their favorite topics; it helps to identify their passion.

Many youths in the All About Business program have earned internships and learned principles through community service and entrepreneurship, putting themselves on a competitive level. One of our kids started going to the program at age 7, selling locks door to door.

Another student from the organization got a job from Apple paying $117,000 with a $72,000 signing bonus. Apple paid for all moving expenses and gave him stock options. Apple had searched his name online and found that he had a history of financial literacy. They saw that he did work in the community and on Facebook, he had started his own company at age 18, and he had several pictures of himself and articles about his projects and activities. He was the perfect example of a student who went to Hampton University, and he landed the same job as a student who went to Harvard.

One student just came back from Paris, where he was learning to be a diplomat. He learned about financial literacy and also taught about it, and when people looked him up online they saw his portfolio. Some students give seminars in local stores—financial literacy workshops—and some write newsletters about financial literacy. These kids and others like them all over the country are making the grade—learning and teaching about financial literacy. They are involved in their communities with an experience level better than most students attending Harvard University, so when they graduate they have an equal chance at success because of their great exposure, hard work, and commitment to win.

Your children might be going to local colleges. These young men and women must work harder to put themselves on a competitive level. For instance, Medgar Evers is a local college in Brooklyn, not on the level of Harvard University, which has a higher competitive edge. An employer, scholarship, or internship will come a lot sooner to a Harvard graduate than it will come to a graduate from Medgar Evers or any other small college. But your children can raise the bar and create their own experiences, possibly by starting a business in your local community. They must create a career portfolio that will compete against a diploma from a better known university.

Credit Cards

When I was in college, everyone in the world wanted to give me a credit card. College students have long been an attractive demographic to banks because they have few financial ties. Banks compete to provide students with credit cards and bank accounts in hopes that they will come back to them when they need mortgages and car loans. Lately, banks have become more aggressive about reaching students through phone calls, emails, and promotions at off-campus locations offering a free gift to sign up. T-shirts are the most common gifts given, but some students even receive iPods when they submit a credit card application.

Fortunately with the new credit card programs—Vanguard—(set up through Obama's administration) it's harder for students to gain access to a credit card. A parent can put the student's name on an account, but then the student is attached to the parent's assets; that can penalize the student by becoming ineligible for grants. A credit card account should primarily be used for a student to establish credit.

If your teenager is college bound, make sure your child knows exactly what a credit card is—how to use it, when to use it, how to read statements, and when to make payments to avoid penalties. Sometimes parents are hesitant to discuss credit with their children because they may be going through personal financial challenges themselves. It's good to teach a child about fiscal responsibility at a young age and, at the same time, it helps parents learn more about the process. Having open discussions about financial literacy is beneficial to both parties.

Student Credit Cards

Several banks are promoting **student credit cards, which** can help students build their credit histories. These cards are actually designed for the 13 to 25 age group and their parents. A student credit card brings newfound freedom, but it also brings new responsibility. It is the college student's responsibility to maintain good standing with the credit card company by paying bills on time and paying more than the minimum payment. An easy way to determine if you are over your head in debt is to examine your spending habits. Warning signs that indicate overspending include:

○ Usually paying only the minimum payment required

○ Making a late payment more than once

○ Meeting and exceeding your credit limit

○ Using one credit card to pay monies due on another credit card

○ Studying less but working more to pay for expenses on your student credit card

Some advice for students starting out in the world is to protect their credit score at all times. Student credit cards can be a benefit and also a major headache, depending on how the credit cards are used. Responsible spenders never use in excess of 50 percent of a credit line; they make all payments on time and pay more than the minimum every month. Students with multiple student credit cards might find the assistance of a credit counselor helpful if they have overextended themselves.

Student credit cards offer great advantages if you pay the balance in full every month. But as students' debt loads have soared along with the cost of college, regulators have become increasingly concerned about the marketing of credit cards to students. More than half of students are now charging books to credit cards, while nearly a quarter are using them to pay tuition. It is best, however, to avoid using your card as a supplemental student loan. Once the introductory rate expires, student credit cards charge a fairly high APR, from 12.99% and up.

If you are looking for a way to teach credit basics to college-bound teens, consider letting them use a low-limit credit card; they will not be able to charge over that set amount. In my opinion, it is far better for teens to learn the ins-and-outs of credit and money management with a low-limit card while still living at home, rather than later, when they are struggling with the demands of college or a first job. The cash back or reward earnings on college student credit cards vary from 1 percent to as high as 5 percent for different types of purchases. To compare credit cards, read through the terms and conditions to determine which card will give your child the highest rewards on frequent expenditures. Some student credit cards even reward points for maintaining a good GPA and paying on time.

While the credit card offers are addressed to the "parents of," the bills and the cards bear the name of the teen, not the parent. Parents serve as co-signers.

The credit limit should be fairly low—$300 to $1,000—so it gives training wheels to the student. It's a good way to learn responsibility. Discuss important topics including interest rates, over the limit charges, and late payment fees, and set some ground rules, such as: Is the card reserved for emergencies or specific purposes such as back-to-school shopping? How much is the teen expected to pay? Then take a step back and let the teen pay the bills. If parents get too involved, the child misses out on the lesson.

Prepaid Debit Cards

A card to be leery of is the prepaid debit card. That industry is built upon a lack of knowledge within the community. Prepaid debit cards are not credit cards. You can't spend money that you haven't already earned; instead, you load funds onto the card and once you've spent that, you can't use the card until you reload. They function just like regular debit or ATM cards, or even like gift cards. Because of this, they can't help you build your credit because they are not technically a credit line.

One distinguishing feature between prepaid cards and standard ATM cards is the fees. Even though free checking is scarcer than it was a few years ago, you can still find a checking account without fees, especially if you can meet the minimum balance requirement. Whatever you do, don't waste your time and money on a prepaid debit card.

Even if you can't meet the minimums and have to pay a fee, few checking accounts charge you for making ATM transactions, adding money to your account, or replacing your card. Prepaid debit cards, on the other hand, charge for any number of incidentals and can easily consume $15 or more each month. That's $180 a year for a card that will probably never hold more than $300 to $500. Prepaid debit cards don't do anything for your credit score. At worst, they'll report bad news, and at best, they won't report anything. A secured credit card, on the other hand, will help create, or rehabilitate, your credit history. Most credit unions that offer secured cards will do so regardless of your FICO score, and even a few reputable national banks offer options with lower fees and better terms. The typical bank offers free debit cards that, if used properly, do not have any fees affiliated with them and can be used for the same purpose as prepaid debit cards.

Scholarships

Before you apply for a student loan, make sure you have exhausted every possible vehicle for obtaining a scholarship. People often overlook local scholarships; these are typically small amounts ranging from $50 to $1,000 being offered by individuals, clubs, organizations, or businesses because they care about the success of young people, they are honoring a loved one, or they wish to promote interest in certain fields of study. Your high school guidance counselor may have some of these applications on file, and you may need to do some sleuthing on your own to track down more local funds. It can seem like a substantial investment of time, but your efforts will likely be rewarded. Begin searching locally when the student is in 10th grade so you have time to create a list of application deadlines and essay requirements.

Much larger scholarships are available, of course, but competition is statewide or national. The book *The African American Scholarship Guide*, published by Amber Classics, includes thousands of top scholarships, grants, and internship programs for African American students, and tips on writing scholarship essays. Another good reference book is *Tom Joyner Presents How to Prepare for College*, which helps you with the admission process and the financial aid process.

Student Loans

Student loans are a special category of consumer loans to be used only for college expenses—tuition, room and board, books, and other supplies. In today's economy it's more important than ever to make sure you borrow wisely by planning for the future and only borrowing what you can afford. When you consider using loans to pay for your college education, think about how you will repay them. Your student loan payments should not be more each year than 8 percent of your annual income at the time of repayment.

It's important to understand the terms of the financial contract. Loans that are federally backed or funded such as Perkins and Stafford/ Direct Loans have fixed interest rates and lower (or no) credit score qualifications for borrowers. If you qualify for Unsubsidized Stafford Student Loans, the government pays the interest while you are in school, saving you money.

Most federal student loans have dollar limits depending on the student's need or year in school. So PLUS loans for parents are beneficial because parents can borrow up to the total cost of attendance (less other financial aid received), either instead of or as a supplement to other student loans.

A *private student loan* is a nongovernment loan made by a private lender based on your credit score. It usually requires a credit-worthy co-signer. *Certified private student loans* require the school to verify that the student is not borrowing more than the total cost of education less other financial aid, before the funds can be applied to the student's account. An *uncertified private student loan* does not require the school to certify the amount borrowed and the funds are usually sent directly to the borrower.

Briefly stated, the financial aid process includes these steps:

1. The family completes the Free Application for Federal Student Aid (FAFSA) and any other forms required by the school.

2. The school sends a financial aid award package, stating the aid being offered.

3. The student and family will accept or decline the aid (all or in part).

4. If student loans are in the award, the student and family will need to apply for each kind of student loan they choose to use.

It will be to your benefit to research many different student loans before applying, and consider the annual percentage rate (APR), the total cost of the loan, the deferment period, and the first payment due date. Confirm details with your lender about interest rates, fees, and borrower benefits, and verify if disbursements are made directly to the school or to the borrower. Ask if the lender uses a "servicer"—a separate company that handles student loan payments and handles customer service questions from borrowers. Find out if the lender will capitalize the interest, which increases the amount owed and the amount of each monthly payment of your student loan. The least expensive option is capitalizing interest only once a year, but some lenders do it every three or six months. Look for a lender with good customer service whom you can reach around the clock and who can present you with options for payment plans.

There are many different kinds of student loans. Here are examples of the order in which they can be used:

1. Always use federally backed or funded student loan types—such as Perkins, Stafford/Direct Loans, and PLUS loans for parents. All of these loans have fixed interest rates and lower (or no) credit score qualifications for borrowers.

    ○ If the school is part of the direct lending program, federal student loans will come from the school

    ○ If the school is not part of the direct lending program, federal student loans will come from a lender

2. If you qualify for Unsubsidized Stafford Student Loans, definitely use those. This means the government pays the interest on the student loan while you are in school, saving you money.

3. PLUS loans for parents are a good option, too, since most federal student loans have limits—students can only borrow specific dollar amounts depending on their need or their year in school. PLUS loans allow the parent of the college student to borrow up to the total cost of attendance (less other financial aid received), either instead of, or as a supplement to other student loans.

Things to Remember about Student Loans

✔ Know all of your student loan options—Investigate many different student loans before applying to get the best student loan or student loans for your needs.

✔ Look beyond the annual percentage rate (APR)—Other factors to consider include the total cost of the loan, how long the deferment period is, and when the first payment is due.

✔ Find a co-signer for private student loans—A student borrower may not be approved without a co-signer, especially younger students without credit histories. And, better rate / fee combinations are usually available only when applying for a student loan with a credit-worthy co-signer.

✔ Confirm loan details with your lender—Ask for confirmation on the interest rates, fees and other loan attributes, such as borrower benefits, with your student loan lender before committing to the loan.

✔ Know how and when the student loan money is disbursed— Confirm if the lender sends the student loan funds to the borrower or if they go to the school directly. Confusion over where the money has gone can delay settling your account. Know how long it will take to process your student loan application.

✔ Ask if the lender uses a servicer—This is a separate company that handles the details of processing and collecting student loan payments, customer service questions from borrowers, originating the loan, and more. Borrowers are often confused when they think they are taking out a loan from Company X, but then get paperwork from Company Y. Communicate with your servicer with questions, address changes or changes to your status as a student.

✔ Find out if the lender will capitalize the interest on the student loan—Some lenders will take the interest that accrues when you are in school and add it to the principal, or the original borrowed amount. This usually only applies to unsubsidized federal student loans and private student loans. Capitalization increases the amount owed and the amount of each monthly payment of your student loan. Some lenders capitalize interest every 3 or 6 months; others once a year. The least expensive option is capitalizing interest only once.

✔ Learn about student loan repayment assistance options— Look for a lender that will help manage your money with options for payment plans and repayment assistance. For example, graduated repayment means your student loan monthly payments start out lower and increase as you earn more money.

✔ Choose a student loan lender with good customer service— Remember that you are the customer—in most cases, you have plenty of options for a lender and student loans are a big commitment. Make sure to find a lender whom you can reach with a toll-free telephone number or fast online assistance available around the clock.

Teach your child about money as early as possible. Include other adults in the conversation so the child understands that everyone cares about their own finances. Help your child find ways to earn money and to be responsible in spending. Explain how a credit score follows you everywhere you go, and that it can either open or close doors for you. By following these principles to teach your children about financial literacy at an early age, they will surely make the grade.

SEVEN WAYS TO MOTIVATE YOUR CHILD ABOUT FINANCIAL LITERACY

1. *Talk to your children about the principles of financial literacy as early as age 6 or 7.*

2. Having open discussions about financial literacy is beneficial to the child, as well as to the parent.

3. Sometimes parents are hesitant to discuss credit with their children because they may be going through personal financial challenges themselves; this is another teaching opportunity.

4. *Getting your children to think about where their money is going can lead to a larger conversation about budgeting before spending.*

5. In the higher grades, when students need it the most, the teachers must teach the students all those things that are necessary to financially sustain them throughout their lives.

6. When many of our students graduate from college they are already in debt, because their parents may not have been able to save for their college education. Learn all your options.

7. From the time they are toddlers, children can learn by playing number games and paying the cashier when purchases are being made at the store.

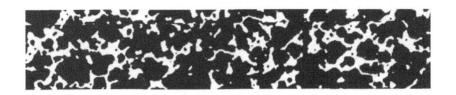

Conclusion

Distinguished Insight

From People Who Have Made the Grade

Who are you? What are you? Maybe you are one tiny speck in an evolving landscape with ever-changing needs and desires. Maybe you are not so tiny. Maybe you are a force to be reckoned with! Think of yourself—your body and mind—as a device. You are a device that can contribute to society, a device that can be used to make the world a better place. No one controls you and the only limitations surrounding you are those you place there yourself.

Your potential is infinite. If you can see it, you can do it. If you conjure up a good idea to set up a business, to start a volunteer program, to help your elderly neighbors, to write a book offering fresh insight—that's what we call *vision*. The vision becomes a dream with a goal. Start taking action on that vision immediately. Jump right in—take baby steps or giant leaps—whatever works for you. Nobody else can bring your vision to fruition like *you* can.

People become successful as a result of actions and choices put into place either for them or by them. Some people have the support and encouragement of their family and community as well as their school and church leaders, in different ways and at different times; other people are on their own and must build themselves up from within. Either way, there are challenges to be overcome.

When people look back over their efforts, they can analyze how they became successful; maybe they can even point to one specific incident that was truly a turning point. They took chances, they believed in themselves, they turned right instead of left, and never looked back.

The distinguished insight that appears in this chapter comes from people in many different careers—people who made the grade and want others to, also. As I look over the bios of these successful people, it seems to me that they have some things in common. They speak of effort, trials, and attitude; they serve on a variety of community action boards and are seen as leaders; they are best-selling authors, which means they are sharing their struggles and lessons to teach others. You will see comments from Olympic and professional athletes, award-winning entertainers, top educators, and respected government officials.

I encourage you to do some research and read their complete biographies and the bios of other successful people so you can learn about their challenges, their turning points, and their success. Their wisdom can help you save some steps on the path you are taking to make the grade.

The Parent:

*To **"make the grade"** one has to be aware of how they are experienced by others. We do not live in this world by ourselves. If our actions and overall attitude towards others are pleasing and bring them joy, it makes for a more rewarding life. It's a world where your success is wanted by more than just yourself.*

—Asadah Kirkland
Author of "Beat Black Kids"

*There are a lot of things that help you **Make the Grade** but above everything it takes belief in yourself. More than anything else, have confidence. There are a lot of people out there who will put you down; but the way to win is to put your trust in your ability because you will need that. I had to overcome a couple of things: being a Latina and the fact that I did not come from money. A lot of my peers, at the time, were sons and daughters of well-off parents. My parents were very giving, loving and always encouraging me, so I never felt disadvantaged even though in a lot of ways we were. As a parent, it's important to encourage your children and give them the proper support.*

—Irene Cara
Honored by the entertainment industry with an Academy Award, two Grammy's, a Golden Globe Actress/dancer/singer/songwriter garnered all of these awards for co-writing and performing "What a Feeling," the title song from the motion picture blockbuster *Flash Dance*.

*I come from a generation of African-Americans where we were always trying to be better and to **Make the Grade**. My father, Dr Roscoe C Brown, Sr, was an official in the United States Public Health Service. I went to the Dunbar High School in Washington, DC, the most competitive high school in the country for blacks. In addition to our academic work, we were very competitive athletically. I was one of the first blacks to play lacrosse. I also played football and basketball. Just as my parents kept my interest peaked and talked to me about new activities, we need to talk to young people*

*about how "It's Cool to Be Smart". We were taught to be very competitive in order to **Make the Grade** throughout life. When I was a young child my parents took me to see the Spirit of St. Louis hanging from the ceiling of the Smithsonian, in Washington, DC and that got me interested in aviation. Then I began to make models of airplanes, and I would fly them with rubber bands. When World War II started, the military began an experimental group that was to be trained in Tuskegee, Alabama. They went to colleges and recruited the best leaders and athletes to be Tuskegee Airmen. At the time, I was in my junior year at Springfield College in Springfield, Massachusetts, where I was valedictorian of my class. Because they had R.O.T.C. when I was in high school, I had already earned a commission as an infantry officer when I was 18-years-old. I resigned my commission, signed up to be a Tuskegee Airman, did my training in Tuskegee, and then got my wings in 1944. I did my combat training in Walterboro, South Carolina, went overseas, and flew combat until the war ended.*

—Doctor Roscoe C. Brown, Jr.

Tuskegee Airman and former squadron commander of the 100th Fighter Squadron of the 332nd Fighter Group, Captain Brown shot down an advanced German Me-262 jet fighter and a FW-190 fighter. He graduated from Springfield College, Springfield, Mass., where he was valedictorian of the Class of 1943. After the war, Captain Brown became a professor at New York University and President of Bronx Community College. In 2007 Brown and the other Tuskegee Airmen collectively, were awarded the Congressional Gold Medal in recognition of their service. Doctor Brown is a member, and past president of the 100 Black Men of America New York Chapter, a professor of Urban Education at the CUNY Graduate Center and a board member of the Make the Grade Foundation.

The Teacher:

I firmly believe our greatest challenge in America today involves the education of our children. Our kids continue to face challenges from both home and classroom that are unprecedented.

Roadblocks to learning are everywhere, yet solutions to improving public education in our inner-cities start with listening to our children. They're speaking louder than ever but most of us don't hear them. However, our own Bob Lee is quite the exception. He's been listening to our children for decades, meeting them in school, on the playground, hosting their dances and sporting events, while encouraging them every step of the way.

From the Bronx to Brooklyn, Newark to Westchester; Bob Lee is a testament to the power of Media when it touches people in the communities they live in.

Bob's **"Make the Grade"** *Foundation is all about accountability, but there's a heck of a lot of fun and learning along the way. Let's take a lesson from the voices of our children and dedicated teachers as told by Bob Lee.*

—Skip Dillard
Operations Manager / Program Director
WBLS/WLIB New York

When you have on the armor of education, you are not only affording yourself power and opportunity, you are also declaring that you have what it takes to make the cut and you will "go hard" for your place in this world. People who know your story will respect you for taking control of your destiny and not allowing your difficult beginnings to dictate the outcome of your life. You will be an asset to your community, which will inspire others who are going through a similar situation and feel they have no way out. Be the one to show them how it's done!

—Ewon Foster
Educator and Author of "The Game Plays You"

*For me, **making the grade** requires you to have a dream you believe in, with a deep passion that comes from your heart. You must be willing to have the discipline to work tirelessly, knowing that the discipline will offer you the freedom to be all that you can be in the future. Finally, you must dare to have the courage to continue when no one else believes in you. It is in these moments that you must dive deep into your spirit to believe in yourself.*

—Erline Belton

Executive coach, author, international consultant and speaker on creating leadership legacy and building organizational infrastructures based on values and truth-telling.

*To **make the grade,** you must have respect for all individuals, show up when you have committed to do so, speak your mind, and always follow through on promises and or commitments.*

—Samuel P. Peabody
Educator /Philanthropist

The Student:

*To **make the grade** in life, it takes preparation and execution. You have to first know what you're getting into through study, then you can execute with confidence, poise and know-how. But without studying what you're doing, you can only be lucky instead of successful. However, luck without a plan will quickly run out, where a plan of success can often be duplicated.*

—**Omar Tyree**
New York Times bestselling author, a 2001 Image Award recipient for Outstanding Literature in Fiction, a 2006 Phillis Wheatley Literary Award winner for Body of Work in Urban Fiction, and a 2010 HBCU Legends Award recipient.

*In order to **make the grade** I suggest the following four things; (1) Read Widely: The Nigerian poet Ben Okri writes: "Read outside your nation, color, class, gender." (2) Never Stop Learning: Continuous learning provides flexibility and options in one's life; (3) Maintain Your Health: Try to get some regular exercise, see your doctor, and don't drink like a fish, or eat like a pig; (4) Always Pursue Your Dreams: Former Apple CEO, Steve Jobs said "...have the courage to follow your heart and intuition. They somehow already know what you truly want to become." Do these things and you will* make the grade *not only in school, but also in life.*

—**Troy Johnson**
President, AALBC.com, LLC

*Our ancestors were right on point when they said, "It takes a village to raise a child". Doctor Bob Lee echoes these sentiments in his book, "**7 Ways to Make the Grade**". In order to effectively educate a child, it demands a multidimensional approach. It requires thinking outside of the status quo, meeting the needs of the students, and empowering them to find their purpose in life. We must help our young people to establish goals and assist them in developing a plan, which will support them in reaching their highest potential. It is crucial that young people understand that "making the grade" is not just about what they achieve today, it is more about how "making the grade" will ultimately impact their tomorrow.*

—**Doctor Arnette F. Crocker, Principal**
Women's Academy of Excellence

◇◇◇

When I was graduating from grammar school, my father wrote a quote from Shakespeare's Hamlet in my yearbook, which has stuck with me forever. It was Polonius' advice to his son Laertes: "This above all to thine own self be true." These wise words served me well as a constant reminder to keep my eye on the lofty academic and spiritual standards I'd set for myself in life, and they especially came in handy at those moments when I was tempted to fall prey to the instant gratification offered by superficial, material pursuits.

—**Kam Williams is a syndicated film and book critic who writes for 100+ publications around the U.S., Europe, Asia, Africa, Canada and the Caribbean. He is a member of the New York Film Critics Online, the Black Film Critics Circle, the NAACP Image Awards Nominating Committee and Rotten Tomatoes. Kam was named Most Outstanding Journalist of the Decade by the Disilgold Soul Literary Review in 2008.**

The Community:

*"**Making the Grade,**" means different things to all of us. To me "**Making the Grade,**" means always doing my best and putting in that extra amount of effort to reach my goals. It's never allowing a setback to influence me more than a day. Staying focused, and being disciplined, even when I don't want to be, always results in a positive outcome. The key to success is never giving up.*
—Sherry Winston
International Jazz Flutist and Recording Artist

If there is something you want to do—go for it. Too many people are not realizing their passion in life because they are "waiting for the right time." If there is something you want to do, the time is now. Don't let anyone tell you that you are too young or too old to **make the grade**. *Talent has no age limit, nor degree requirement.*
—Pat Stevenson
Publisher, Harlem News Group, Inc.

*To **make the grade**, I would tell kids to go to school, reach for the moon and at least you'll land among the stars. I am the winning professional drag racer, a 9-time world champion and I've always had my own drag racing team. I've been doing this for 27 years and I was the first African American to break through the color barrier. It took a lot for me because people kept writing in to see what was going on, but I kept winning. It was hard in the beginning—I didn't have anyone—my father died when I was five—my mother also died when I was young. When I was 18, I decided to give it a year. In 1998, I was in the right place at the right time when I became the first and only African American to win…and I am still the only one. When I was going to school, I didn't have a dream to be a racer. I have been told that it's important to be diverse and not put all my eggs in one basket; so I also have a trucking company and a drag racing school.*
—Ricky Gadson
Motorcycle Drag Racer

*There's a few ways to **make the grade:** Have the proper attitude. Stay in school. Have the ability to appreciate things and say Thank you when the need arises.*

—Former Congressman Ed Towns
U.S. Representative for New York's 10th Congressional District, Serving since 1983, and the former Chairman of the House Oversight and Government Reform Committee.

*To **make the grade,** there are two lessons I would definitely learn: The rules of the training camp and how to stay focused. Know what you have, know what you want and know the quality of people you surround yourself with. No matter where you come from, you should prioritize your brain power.*

—Kris Aman
VP/General Manager, Nike

The Clergy:

*To **make the grade**, you must pray. You can't allow yourself to get in the way of what God has intended for you. They don't want you to pray in school, but I think you have to have a strong connection with God. You must have a good understanding that you can make it, but you have to do it through hard work and continuous efforts. Have confidence within yourself and faith in God.*

—Andrew Young
Politician, diplomat, activist and pastor from Georgia. He has served as Mayor of Atlanta, a Congressman from the 5th district, and United States Ambassador to the United Nations. He served as President of the National Council of Churches USA, was a member of the Southern Christian Leadership Conference (SCLC) during the 1960s Civil Rights Movement, and was a supporter and friend of Doctor Martin Luther King, Jr.

*To **make the grade** you've got to have faith in God and yourself. Faith—the trusting belief that your best future is in God's hands. You have options in making the grade. However, always, always choose the options that will lead to your best future, which is in God. Then, work hard for making the grade, trusting God for the success that only comes through Him and hard work.*

—Dr. Warren H. Stewart, Sr.
Pastor, the First Institutional Baptist Church, Phoenix, AZ. Author of "VICTORY TOGETHER FOR MARTIN LUTHER KING, JR.: The Story of Dr. Warren H. Stewart, Sr., Governor Evan Mecham and the Historic Battle for a Martin Luther King, Jr. Holiday in Arizona"

*When it comes to **making the grade**, there are no college courses to build up self-esteem or high school or elementary school. I'm for people bettering themselves, no matter who they are and where they are, doing all they can to be all they can be. If you don't get those values at an early age, nurtured in your home, you don't get them. There are many things I would have done differently, I submit to God's sovereignty and His purpose in my life and I thank Him that He brought me the way He brought me and gave me what He gave me when He thought I could handle it.*

—**Bishop Thomas Dexter "T. D." Jakes, Sr.**
Pastor of The Potter's House, a multiracial, nondenominational church with 50-plus active outreach ministries, Ministerial and business visionary, entrepreneurial trailblazer, altruistic philanthropist, and spiritual shepherd to millions around the globe. Author of "Woman, Thou Art Loosed", the first of many best-selling books

The Health Component:

*To **make the grade**, you must have a dream. Stay within your bounds and let your passion take over. Your health can affect your ability to fulfill your dreams. To make the grade and stay healthy, one of the things I would be concerned with is high blood sugar count or low blood sugar count. I played baseball for about 18 years with diabetes. I was about 23 when I was diagnosed. It's something that sneaks up on you. I actually went blind for about a week and I went to the doctor and discovered that I had a high blood sugar count of about 800. The doctor said to me, "If you don't get your blood count down you are gone." That's the reality with a lot of people. There aren't any symptoms, until it's full blown. Sometimes people feel bad and think maybe tomorrow I'll feel better. But it sneaks up on you, so don't ignore it when you feel bad—it can happen at any age. Stay healthy and always think about fair play, sports have a way of governing you; so if it's your passion, let it define you. When that happens, know the limit of where you can go.*

—Lou Brock
A distinguished member of the most elite organization in baseball, the National Baseball Hall of Fame. This prestigious honor has been achieved by only one percent of the more than 20,000 players in the history of Major League Baseball.

*To **make the grade**, it takes hard work and dedication. No partying, no hanging out, no drinking, no drugs and no smoking.*

—Mark Breland
5-time Golden Glove Champ Olympic Gold Medalist
2-time Welterweight Champion of the World

Financial Literacy:

To ***make the grade,*** *it is imperative that the Black community scrutinize our spending patterns as excessive consumption continues to present a serious problem within our communities. Over 93% of our dollars are spent on consumption (compared to 85% of all dollars in America spent on consumption); we invest 20% less than whites per month; and our net worth as a community continues to remain 20% of the net worth of our white counterparts. The unnecessary excessive fees related to the pre-paid debit ca* do nothing but compound the problem by eroding crucial capital that could be used for other important activities such as retirement, entrepreneurship endeavors, higher education costs, home ownership, and/or building a sound financial legacy for our families.*

—Ryan Mack
Author of *"Living in the Village: Build Your Financial Future and Strengthen Your Community"*, As an advocate of philanthropy Ryan Mack has worked diligently within the community and beyond to increase financial awareness.

◇◇◇

*In order to **make the grade**, you must first realize that Success is the gift you already have. A person has to remember that the road to success is always under construction. Growth is a series of mistakes. That's the only way you learn. Failure is a great teacher, and I think when you make mistakes and when you recover from them and you treat them as valuable learning experience, then you've got something to share. The most successful people in this world recognize that taking chances to get what they want is much more productive than sitting around being too scared to take a shot. The two most important days in your life are the day you are born and the day you know why.*

—Broderick Steven "Steve" Harvey
Comedian, television host, radio personality, actor, and author. He hosts The Steve Harvey Morning Show, Steve Harvey, and Family Feud. He is the author of *"Act Like a Lady, Think Like a Man"*, *"Straight Talk, No Chaser: How to Find and Keep a Man"* and *"Act Like a Success, Think Like a Success: Discovering Your Gift and the Way to Life's Riches"*.

Do You Think You Can Transform Anyone?

A man can be as great as he wants to be. If you believe in yourself and have the courage, the determination, the dedication, the competitive drive and if you are willing to sacrifice the little things in life and pay the price for the things that are worthwhile, it can be done.

—*Vince Lombardi*

Whenever I am asked, "Do you think you can transform anyone?" I say, "ABSOLUTELY!"

In order to make changes, in order to transform our youth, people need to realize that we must do this together—communities should come together and move in one direction. In my experimenting with the microscope, everything came together to make a special mix. When I was covering the September 11th terrorist attacks for the radio station, many nations of people came together. Everyone was on the same page. We went into Afghanistan and Iraq and did what was necessary at a time of sympathy.

When young people get shot, it is a time when communities come together. But, we can't always wait for something tragic to happen. We have to move together in one direction all the time. We must come together again, just like everyone did when I was growing up, as a community in order to help our young people.

I have come through much adversity and overcome many challenges. Driving alone through the desert into an unknown darkness was an adversity; being told by my boss at the print shop that I would

147

be a failure when I quit my job was an adversity. There were numerous instances that could have led me astray. But, the community of people whom I encountered along the way upheld all those things in my life that could have turned me in the wrong direction. Some held my hand, some patted me on the back, some gave me strong advice, and some led by example.

You will be coming through many adversities in your lifetime—negative things that can hold you back—but don't allow those situations to interfere with your journey. Stay positive, stay strong, be successful and you will, without a doubt, Make the Grade.

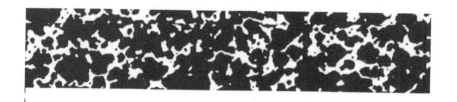

About the Author

DOCTOR BOB LEE

Bob Lee, also known as Doctor Bob Lee, began his career in 1979 after receiving his BA and MA in Communications from New York Institute of Technology, where he was a DJ for 88.7 WTNY Radio. Lee later advanced to music director, program director and eventually general manager of WTNY Radio. In 1980, Lee joined WBLS for a one-year internship before moving on to KISS-FM for his start in commercial broadcasting. He thereafter returned to WBLS where he has had a rich and diverse career. From 1986 to 1994, Lee was a DJ on the weekend edition of WBLS's renowned program *The Quiet Storm*, and for several years provided live reports on the morning show from various WBLS-sponsored community events.

The "Doctor" is on the air at 107.5 WBLS - Your Number One Source for R & B every Monday through Friday from midnight until 5 a.m. Lee has interviewed such musical greats as Stevie Wonder, Patti LaBelle, Luther Vandross, Jaheim, Mariah Carey, Mary J. Blige, Kenny "Baby Face" Edmonds, the O'Jays, Wynton Marsalis, Whitney Houston, P. Diddy, and Jill Scott, among many others. He can also be heard on air every day with his *Daily Dose* series tackling health issues that affect the community.

In addition to his on-air roles, Lee is the community affairs director for WBLS. As part of his community-based work, Lee has developed strong ties to many local and national politicians and public figures, including former President Clinton, former New York Mayor Michael Bloomberg, former New York Mayor David Dinkins, and former Bronx Borough President Adolfo Carrión.

As part of Senator Hillary Clinton's 911 initiative/Commission, Lee participated in a phone conference every other week on how to better serve the community during an emergency. Lee was also a panelist and speaker for a Healing our Community, "My Brother's Keeper initiative", which is President Barack Obama's multimillion-dollar initiative to boost young minority men and boys.

Lee hosts the weekly live television program *Open*, which broadcasts on BronxNet, a cable television station serving the Bronx and upper Manhattan. The program features news and topics affecting the Bronx community and also treats viewers to new and established musical guests.

Lee also appears frequently in the Harlem community as the host of live music and other events, such as Harlem Summer Stage and classic soul programs at the Apollo Theater featuring Regina Belle and Jeffrey Osborne. In addition, his strong ties to the community are reflected in his many charitable endeavors. He is involved in corporate speaking and promotional work for businesses with an interest in the welfare of the community. Lee also helps college students interested in radio careers by serving as a mentor for *Table for Two*, a weekly music program that broadcasts from WLIU 88.1 FM radio in Brooklyn and is staffed by interns from Long Island University.

Among his other activities, Lee is a founder and board member of the Make the Grade Foundation, a not-for-profit organization that provides mentoring and aid to school children. He has received numerous awards from mayors, borough presidents, city council members, senators, and assemblymen, as well as proclamations from organizations and schools in the tri-state area. *You Can Make the Grade* is his first published book.

Learn more about Doctor Bob Lee online at DoctorBobLee. com and WBLS.com. For further information about Make the Grade Foundation or to purchase Books for your organization in bulk, email: BobLee@makethegrade.org or bobleewbls@gmail.com

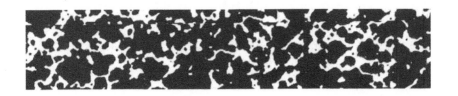

Appendixes

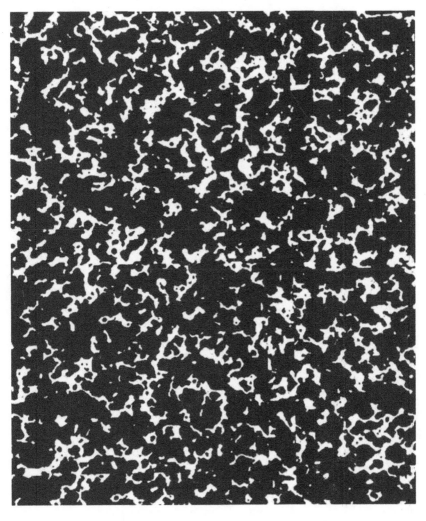

Appendixes

Bob Lee

Doctor Bob Lee
http://www.doctorboblee.com
Bob Lee's personal site contains his bio, gallery, wide range of experience and services.

http://www.facebook.com/makethegrade
http://www.facebook.com/DoctorBobLee
http://www.facebook.com/BobLee
http://www.twitter.com/DoctorBobLee

107.5 WBLS
http:/www.wbls.com
Your Number One Source for R & B

Scholarships

AFRICAN AMERICAN STUDENTS ARE NOT APPLYING FOR SCHOLARSHIPS:

Even if you do not have a college-aged child at home; please share this with someone who does, and to anyone and everyone that comes to mind. Though there are a number of companies and organizations that have donated money for scholarships to African Americans, a great deal of the money is being returned because of a lack of interest or awareness.

No one is going to knock on our doors and ask if we can use a scholarship.

Take the initiative to get your children involved! Money shouldn't be returned to donating companies because we fail to apply for it.

Please pass this information on to family members, nieces, nephews, and friends with children. We must get the word out that money is available. If you are a college student or preparing to become one, you probably already know how useful additional money can be.

1. BELL LABS FELLOWSHIPS FOR UNDER REPRESENTED MINORITIES
   http://www.alcatel-lucent.com/wps/portal/BellLabs

2. Student Inventors Scholarships http://www.invent.org/collegiate http://www.invent.org/collegiate/

3. Student Video Scholarships
   http://www.christophers.org/vidcon2k.html

4. Coca-Cola Two Year College Scholarships
   http://www.coca-colascholars.org/programs.html

5. Holocaust Remembrance Scholarships
   http://holocaust.hklaw.com/

6. Ayn Rand Essay Scholarships
   http://www.aynrand.org/contests/

7. Brand Essay Competition
   http://www.instituteforbrandleaders hip.org/
   IBLEssayContest-2002Rules.htm

8. Gates Millennium Scholarships (major)
   http://www.gmsp.org/nominationmaterials/read.
   dbm?ID=12

9. Xerox Scholarships for Students
   http://www2.xeroxcom/go/xrx/about_xerox/about_xerox_
   detail.jsp

10. Sports Scholarships and Internships
    http://www.ncaa.org/about/scholarships.html

11. National Assoc. of Black Journalists Scholarships (NABJ)
    http://www.nabj.org/html/studentsvcs.html

12. Saul T. Wilson Scholarships (Veterinary)
    http://www.aphis.usda.gov/mb/mrphr/jobs/stw.html

13. Thurgood Marshall Scholarship Fund
    http://www.thurgoodmarshallfund.org/sk_v6.cfm

14. FinAid: The Smart Students Guide to Financial Aid schol-
    arships)
    http://www.finaid.org/

15. Presidential Freedom Scholarships
    http://www.nationalservice.org/scholarships/

16. Microsoft Scholarship Program
http://www.microsoft.com/college/scholarships/minority.asp

17. Wired Scholar Free Scholarship Search
http://www.wiredscholar.com/paying/scholarship_search/pay_scholarship _search.jsp

18. Hope Scholarships Lifetime Credits
http://www.ed.gov/inits/hope/

19. William Randolph Hearst Endowed Scholarship for Minority Students
http://www.apsanet.org/PS/grants/aspen3.cfm

20. Multiple List of Minority Scholarships
http://gehon.ir.mia mi.edu/financial-assistance/Scholarship/black.html

21. Guaranteed Scholarships
http://www.guaranteed-scholarships.com/

22. BOEING scholarships (some HBCU connects)
http://www.boeing.com/companyoffices/educationrelations/scholarships

23. Easley National Scholarship Program
http://www.naas.org/senior.htm

24. Maryland Artists Scholarships
http://www.maef.org/

25. Jacki Tuckfield Memorial Graduate Business Scholarship (for AA students in South Florida)
http://wwwjackituckfield.org/

26. Historically Black College & University Scholarships
http://www.iesabroad.org/info/hbcu.htm

27. Actuarial Scholarships for Minority Students
http://www.beanactuary.org/minority/scholarships.htm

28. International Students Scholarships Aid Help
    http://www.iefa.org/

29. College Board Scholarship Search
    http://apps.collegeboard.com/cbsearch_ss/welcome.jsp

30. Burger King Scholarship Pro gram
    http://www.bkscholars.csfa.org/

31. Siemens Westinghouse Competition
    http://www.siemens-foundationorg/

32. GE and LuLac Scholarship Funds
    http://www.lulac.org/Programs/Scholar.html

33. CollegeNet's Scholarship Database
    http://mach25.collegenet.com/cgi-bin/M25/index

34. Union Sponsored Scholarships and Aid
    http://www.aflcioorg/scholarships/scholar.htm

35. Federal Scholarships Aid Gateways 25 Scholarship
    Gateways from Black Excel
    http://www.blackexcel.org/25scholarships.htm

36. Scholarship Financial Aid Help
    http://www.blackexcel.org/fin-sch.htm

37. Scholarship Links (Ed Finance Group)
    http://www.efg.net/link_scholarship.htm

38. FAFSA On The Web (Your Key Aid Form Info)
    http://www.fafsa.ed.gov/

39. Aid Resources For Re-Entry Students
    http://www.back2college.com/

40. Scholarships and Fellowships
    http://www.osc.cuny.edu/sep/links.html

41. Scholarships for Study in Paralegal Studies
    http://www.paralegals.org/Choice/2000west.htm

42. HBCU Packard Sit Abroad Scholarships (for study around the world)
http://www.sit.edu/studyabroad/packard_nomination.html

43. Scholarship and Fellowship Opportunities
http://ccmi.uchicag o.edu/schl1.html

44. INROADS internships
http://www.inroads.org/

45. ACT-SO bEURoeOlympics of the Mind 'A Scholarships
http://www.naacp.org/work/actso/act-so.shtml

46. Black Alliance for Educational Options Scholarships
http://www.baeo.org/options/privatelyfinanced.jsp

47. ScienceNet Scholarship Listing
http://www.sciencenet.emory.edu/undergrad/scholarships.html

48. Graduate Fellowships For Minorities Nationwide
http://cuinfo.cornell.edu/Student/GRFN/list.phtml?category=MINORITIES

49. RHODES SCHOLARSHIPS AT OXFORD
http://www.rhodesscholar.org/info.html

50. The Roothbert Scholarship Fund
http://www.roothbertfund.org/schol

Resources

FastWeb

http://fastweb.com

(FastWeb, the Internet's leading scholarship search service, helps students make the decisions that shape their lives: choosing a college, paying for college, and finding jobs and internships.)

Scholarships.com

http://www.scholarships.com

(College financial aid at Scholarships.com, college scholarship search with our free online college scholarship search. Financial aid, education loans.)

FinAid

http://finaid.org/scholarships

(FinAid's Guide to Scholarships includes information about the best free scholarship searches, unusual scholarships, and prestigious scholarships.)

Scholarshiphelp.org
http://scholarshiphelp.org

(The goal of this website is to educate students about scholarship access and the necessary requirements for achieving maximum financial aid.)

HBCUs

http://hbcuconnect.com

(Free information and services for the HBCU community; including enrolled and prospective students, parents, faculty and alumni.)

UNCF

http://www.uncf.org

(UNCF provides operating funds and technology enhancement services for 39 member historically black colleges and universities (HBCUs), scholarships and internships for students at about 900 institutions and faculty and administrative professional training.)

NYC Schools

schools.nyc.gov
http://schools.nyc.gov

(Official site of the public education system in the five boroughs, with search functions by borough, district, and street.)

New York State Education Department

www.emsc.nysed.gov
(New York State Education Department, Albany New York.)

NYC Local Schools

www.localschooldirectory.com

(Over 130,000 schools are listed including pre-kindergarten, kindergarten, elementary schools, middle schools and high schools. We statistically break down school information at the state, city, district and individual school levels.)

NY Metro Parents

www.nymetroparents.com

(This website features cutting-edge search capabilities to seek out New York City family-related businesses and services, and activities. The search engine enables users to access the NYMetroParents.com Guide to the Web, the web's largest parenting web link database.)

You Can Go to College

www.youcangotocollege.net

For students 9th to 12th grades-SAT prep and college tours

Let's help our Youth!